MW00996558

Griffon Spitfire Aces

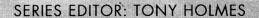

SERIES EDITOR: TONY HOLMES

OSPREY AIRCRAFT OF THE ACES • 81

Griffon Spitfire Aces

Andrew Thomas

OSPREY
PUBLISHING

First published in Great Britain in 2008 by Osprey Publishing
Midland House, West Way, Botley, Oxford OX2 0PH, UK
44-02 23rd St, Suite 219, Long Island City, NY 11101, USA
Email: info@ospreypublishing.com

Osprey Publishing is part of the Osprey Group.

Transferred to digital print on demand 2012

First published 2008
3rd impression 2010

Printed and bound by Cadmus Communications, USA

CIP Data for this publication is available from the
British Library

ISBN: 978 1 84603 298 1

Edited by Tony Holmes
Page design by Tony Truscott
Cover Artwork by Mark Postlethwaite
Aircraft Profiles by Chris Davey
Scale Drawings by Mark Styling
Index by Alan Thatcher
Typeset in Adobe Garamond and Univers

The Woodland Trust
Osprey Publishing is supporting the Woodland Trust, the
UK's leading woodland conservation charity, by funding
the dedication of trees.

www.ospreypublishing.com

Front Cover
By early April 1945, No 41 Sqn, which formed part of No
125 Wing of the 2nd Tactical Air Force (TAF), was based
at the Dutch airfield of Twente, to which it had moved
a week earlier. The unit was led by Sqn Ldr J B Shepherd,
an ace with two and three shared victories to his name.
He had assumed command on 18 March following the
disbandment of No 610 Sqn, with whom he had destroyed
seven V1 flying bombs the previous summer. Under
John Shepherd's leadership, No 41 Sqn continued
marauding over the shrinking territory of the Third Reich
on daily armed reconnaissance missions at low and
medium altitude. At such heights, the unit's superb
Griffon-engined Spitfire XIVs were superior to the
piston-engined fighters fielded by the Luftwaffe.

Early on the evening of 14 April, Shepherd led Red
Section on a patrol, although his flight of four aircraft was
soon down to three when one of the pilots was forced to
return to base with engine trouble. The remaining trio of
Spitfires flew on to the Bremen area, where, on the second
leg of their sweep shortly after 1930 hrs, they approached
Nordholz airfield at 7000 ft. A pair of enemy aircraft that had
just taken off were quickly spotted, the leading machine
being a Bf 110 nightfighter from 7./NJG 3. It was towing a
Me 163 Komet of II./JG 400, piloted by Oberfeldwebel
Werner Nelte (a seven-victory ace who had flown on the
Eastern Front with 1./JG 54). The rocket fighter was being
towed to the unit's new base at Husum, on the
Schleswig-Holstein peninsula. Other Me 163s had been
flown there under their own power earlier that same day.

On sighting the enemy, Sqn Ldr Shepherd immediately
led his section down, as he recounted afterwards in his
Combat Report;

'I recognised them as an Me 163, being towed by an
Me 110. I was closing very rapidly, but managed to get a
short burst in on the Me 110, obtaining strikes on the port
engine and cockpit. The Me 110 went into a left-hand
diving turn, flipping onto its back and crashing into a field,
whereupon it burst into flames.

'The Me 163 appeared to break away from the Me 110
and make a wide left turn, before finally diving straight in
about three fields away from the Me 110.'

In fact Werner Nelte managed to pull the Me 163 out of
its dive at the last moment and crash-land, although the
towing crew were killed when their Bf 110 crashed in
flames. The brief combat was witnessed by Shepherd's
No 3, Flt Lt A W Jolly, who confirmed his CO's claim for
two victories. Shepherd thus became the only RAF pilot to
be credited with the destruction of a Komet, albeit not
when under rocket power.

Shepherd led No 41 Sqn with distinction until VE-Day,
achieving six more victories. These kills made him the
fourth most successful pilot on the Griffon-engined Spitfire.

This specially commissioned painting by Mark
Postlethwaite shows John Shepherd's Spitfire flying past
the burning Bf 110 as it dives to its destruction, whilst
Nelte performs a crash-landing in his powerless Komet

CONTENTS

A NEW FORCE

During late evening of 17 April 1943, a Spitfire from No 41 Sqn took off from its base at Hawkinge, on the Kent Channel coast, for a 'Jim Crow' patrol that would see its pilot looking for coastal shipping to attack off the enemy-held coast between Calais and Ostend some 20 miles away. The post-flight Combat Report submitted by the Spitfire's pilot, Flg Off Dickie Hogarth, read as follows;

'Slight flak came from points on the west side of Dunkirk. I saw a small ship in Ostend as I passed, so I went into a steep turn to port to look at the vessel again more closely. I was about two miles north of Ostend, flying at 320 mph IAS (indicated air speed) at 200 ft. Halfway round my turn I saw a Ju 88 painted black crossing my path from port to starboard. In a second I found myself right on his tail, so I pressed the button for a ten-second burst, closing rapidly from about 500 yards to just 10 yards. I was missing behind, but hit the tail and I think the fuselage. The tail crumpled up, and I broke off to starboard and made a quarter attack closing to astern, firing about 2-3 seconds of machine gun ammunition – all that I had left.

'Allowing quarter ring deflection on this attack, I set fire to his port engine. He then glided down into the sea, burning well on the port side. I was hit by fire from one rear machine gun, and had about three or four bullets pass through the wing. This did not affect the flying qualities of my aircraft, however, and I subsequently returned to Hawkinge and pancaked at 2100 hrs.'

Hogarth was flying EN235 – one of the newly delivered Spitfire XIIs fitted with a powerful Rolls-Royce Griffon III engine producing 1735 hp at 1000 ft. He had just claimed the Griffon-engined Spitfire's first victory. No 41 Sqn had begun re-equipping with this potent new fighter

The Griffon-engined Spitfire's first operational sortie was an uneventful scramble on 3 April 1943, led by Flg Off 'Jumbo' Birbeck, who would subsequently make five claims with the Mk XII, including two destroyed (*No 41 Sqn records*)

The Spitfire XII married the Mk V airframe with a Griffon engine that was housed in a re-contoured nose. With clipped wings, the Mk XII retained the elegance of the early Spitfire variants, and proved a formidable low altitude fighter (*author's collection*)

The first pilot lost on operations in the Spitfire XII was Flt Lt Rex Poynton of No 41 Sqn, who was shot down by Fw 190s from JG 26 on 24 April 1943. The German pilots involved in this action claimed that they had downed an RAF Mustang (*No 41 Sqn records*)

The first production Spitfire XII was EN221, which was test flown by the Intensive Flying Development Flight (IFDF). The aircraft later served with No 41 Sqn (*via Wojtek Matusiak*)

optimised for low-level operations while based at Llanbedr, on the west coast of Wales, with the first example (EN228) having been delivered to the unit on 24 February.

After a brief working up, No 41 Sqn flew the type's first operational sorties on 3 April when, at 1600 hrs, Flg Off 'Jumbo' Birbeck in EN601 and Sgt J Stonier in EN609 were scrambled from Valley, although they found nothing. Ten days later the squadron moved south to Hawkinge, and 48 hours after that, on the 15th, the Spitfire XII made its operational debut over occupied Europe when 'A' Flight commander Flt Lt Rex Poynton, in EN601, led a patrol over Dieppe. Eight days later, again while flying off Dieppe, Poynton failed to return from a mission in this aircraft, which duly became the first Griffon-engined Spitfire to be lost on operations.

A MARRIAGE OF NECESSITY

The development of the Rolls-Royce Griffon and the eclipse of the Spitfire V by the Focke-Wulf Fw 190 resulted in the marriage of the older airframe with a powerful new engine as a counter to the Luftwaffe's increasing superiority in the low-level environment. Featuring clipped wings, a re-contoured nose to house the new engine and a four-bladed propeller, the interim Mk XII was very much optimised for the low-level intercept role. This made the fighter ideal for countering the increasing number of enemy attacks on south coast towns.

The first Spitfire to be fitted with a Griffon engine was the experimental prototype DP485, which had originally been a Mk III. Following a series of modifications, it became the prototype of the first Griffon-engined production variant, designated the Mk XII. The aircraft completed its first flight with Griffon power on 27 November 1941.

The first true Mk XII was EN221, which made its maiden flight with Flt Lt Clive Gosling at the controls on 13 October 1942. The fighter was duly sent to A&AEE (Aeroplane & Armament Experimental Establishment) Boscombe Down for testing in early November. Soon joined by EN222,

both Spitfires were tested by the Intensive Flying Development Flight at Supermarine's Experimental Flight Test airfield at High Post, near Salisbury. Amongst those to fly the aircraft were Polish aces Flt Lt Henryk Pietrzak and Flt Lt Wladislaw Potoki. The evaluation testing continued until February 1943.

Just 100 Mk XIIs were built, as the next Griffon-engined variant in the form of the Spitfire XIV then came on line. This mark, too, was an interim solution, pending development of the definitive Mk XVIII.

The Spitfire Mk XIV was a combination of the Mk VIII airframe, albeit much modified, and the Griffon 65 engine of 2050 hp that drove a five-bladed airscrew. This variant was intended for both high and low altitude operations, hence the engine/airscrew combination. The Griffon 65 was fitted with a two-speed supercharger and an intercooler, and to offset the fighter's lengthened nose, the fin area was also increased. This and other aerodynamic improvements greatly improved the lateral control for pilots flying the Mk XIV. The aircraft could be fitted with either a type B wing, mounting two 20 mm cannon and four 0.303-in Browning machine guns, or the type E wing, with two 20 mm cannon and a pair of 0.50-in Browning machine guns. Thus fitted, the Mk XIV's operational weight with full fuel and ammunition was 8400 lbs – considerably more than the 5300 lbs of the original Spitfire I!

At the IFDF at High Post, the first two Spitfire XIIs were evaluated by Polish pilots Flt Lts Wladislaw Potoki (left) and Henryk Pietrzak, both of whom already had several victories. They later became aces. (*Pietrzak family via W Matusiak*)

The Spitfire XIV's beefed up features, including the extended nose with massive five-bladed propeller and the new tail contours, are readily apparent in this excellent view of the first production aircraft, RB140, which later served with No 610 Sqn (*P H T Green Collection*)

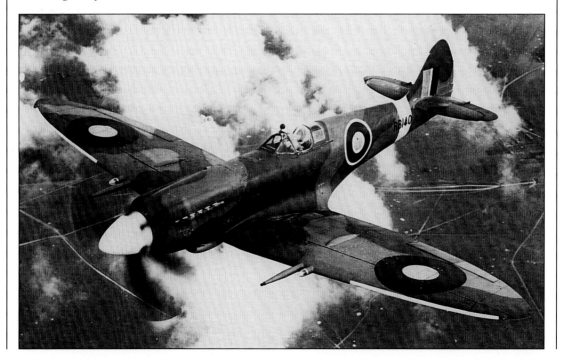

injuries (author's collection)

Prototype testing was conducted on several converted Spitfire VIIIs, the first of which flew in January 1943. They boasted several aerodynamic modifications, including the larger fin and the moving inboard of the ailerons in an effort to improve lateral stability.

The Mk XIV was highly regarded by those who flew it. One pilot who met with success, including the destruction of an enemy jet, was Flt Lt Derek Rake of No 41 Sqn, who recalled for this volume his views on the aircraft and its engine;

'The take off in the Mk XIV was a bit different to the earlier Merlin-powered Spits in that the power of the Griffon meant that you had to use full rudder and even aileron to counteract the torque, and so stay on the narrow PSP (pierced-steel planking) strips on take-off. We had to limit the boost to about +8 lbs until we were off the ground. Thereafter, we had to get used to adjusting the trim as we changed power and/or speed in the range of up to +18 lbs. This was of course particularly important when firing either air-to-air or air-to-ground, as speed increased or decreased. Any skidding played havoc with accuracy.

'It was always comforting to me to know that the increased power of the Griffon would enable me to turn inside and/or out climb a Bf 109 or Fw 190. We did find, however, that the latest Fw 190D could get away from us by rolling on its back and going vertically downwards. In an attempt to combat this manoeuvre, we were allowed to increase the boost to +21 lbs. To do this we had to push the throttle through a thin piece of piano wire. The only time I tried this, when attempting to catch up with an Fw 190D in a dive, there was a tremendous clatter and my Spit felt as if it was going to shake itself to pieces. I managed to keep the engine going by throttling right back – using just enough power to limp back to Volkel. It transpired that a con-rod had come through the side of the engine. It was confidence building to realise how robustly the Griffon was built.

'Another time – the day of the crossing of the Rhine on 24 April 1945 – we started the day at first light at 25,000 ft, trying to ensure that the Luftwaffe's Me 262s did not dive-bomb our troops crossing the river. Later in the day we were down at low level looking for German tanks in a wood. I was hit in the port wing by ground fire and again had heavy vibration in the engine. After landing back at Volkel without any flaps or brakes, I discovered that one blade of the five-bladed propeller had been shot off. What an engine!'

DEFENDING THE REALM

As No 41 Sqn (led by 16- victory Hurricane ace Sqn Ldr Tom Neil) began its operations over the Channel, a second unit commenced re-equipment with the Griffon-engined Mk XII. Based at Honiley for the conversion, No 91 'Nigeria' Sqn, led by Sqn Ldr Ray Harries, who already had three and three shared victories to his credit, received its first aircraft (EN613) just five days after Flg Off Hogarth had opened the Mk XII's combat account. A few more arrived in early May 1943, with no less than seven

The first Griffon Spitfire unit was No 41 Sqn, which was led by 23-year-old ace Sqn Ldr Tom 'Ginger' Neil. He had gained a total of 16 victories during the Battle of Britain and the defence of Malta (*T F Neil via B Cull*)

flying in on the 13th. By 18 May No 91 Sqn had 18 Spitfire XIIs on strength, and it returned to Hawkinge with 12 of them three days later. No 41 Sqn had suffered several casualties by then, and it fell to No 91 Sqn to achieve the Spitfire XII's first major success against the Luftwaffe.

Since early 1943, German aircraft had been attacking towns along the south coast with fast, low-flying Fw 190 fighter-bombers, often arriving at dusk, or using bad visibility or weather as cover. These pin-prick 'tip and run' attacks did cause some damage and casualties, but they led to a disproportionate effort to counter them, including generating costly standing patrols. It was in part to counter this threat that the two Spitfire XII squadrons were immediately based on the south coast.

During his time with No 41 Sqn, Neil's usual mount was Spitfire XII EN237/EB-V, which was eventually wrecked in a landing accident at Lympne in March 1944 (*T F Neil via W Matusiak*)

As dusk fell on the evening of 25 May, a raid by an estimated 15 hostiles was detected heading towards Folkestone just as the CO in EN625/DL-K and Plt Off Johnny Round in EN624 landed at Hawkinge at the end of an uneventful low-level standing patrol off Hastings. Just behind them were Free Frenchman Flg Off Jean Maridor in MB832/DL-S and Plt Off Dave Davy in EN623/DL-N. The four of them roared away towards the enemy formation of Fw 190s from SKG 10, which scattered and dropped their bombs as they approached. Extracts from Raymond Harries' Combat Report described his squadron's first action with the Griffon Spitfire;

'I was leading Blue Section on a defensive patrol. I had just returned to base, and with my No 2, had just landed when the scramble signal was given from the watch office. We both immediately took off again, and saw enemy aircraft approaching Folkestone.

'I immediately dived towards the sea, the enemy aircraft turning back and jettisoning their bombs as soon as they saw us. Going over Folkestone, I experienced very heavy flak – fortunately inaccurate(!) – from our ground defences. I sighted one lone Fw 190 at sea level returning to France. I came in from his starboard side, delivering a three-second burst at 250 yards. The enemy aircraft hit the sea tail first, split in two and sank immediately.'

In claiming his eighth victory (thought to have been Fw 190A-5 wk-nr 2511 of 6./SKG 10, flown by Oberleutnant Josef Keller), Harries had opened his squadron's Spitfire XII account, but more followed, as his Combat Report continued;

'I then spotted another Fw 190 to starboard. I flew straight over the top of it in order to identify it in the failing light. The enemy aircraft pulled up his nose and gave me a quick squirt. I pulled straight up to about

The second Spitfire XII unit was No 91 Sqn, under the command of Sqn Ldr Ray Harries. He eventually became the most successful Griffon-Spitfire pilot, achieving 10.5 victories with the fighter. Harries survived the war with an overall score of 15 and 3 shared kills (*P J Hart*)

Flg Off Jean Maridor claimed the first of his two Fw 190 kills with this aircraft (MB832/DL-S) on 25 May 1943. As this photograph clearly shows, the aircraft was all but destroyed in a crash at Hamble on 6 June. Sent to Air Service Training for a total rebuild, it did not return to No 91 Sqn until 3 January 1944. It was lost 20 days later when Flt Sgt J Hymas was shot down by German fighters on 'Ramrod 472' (*J D Oughton*)

Sqn Ldr Ray Harries' first two
Spitfire XII successes came on
25 May 1943 when at the controls
of EN625/DL-K. Later in the year,
future V1 ace Flg Off Ray Nash
achieved two victories with this
aircraft as well (*R A McPhie*)

1000 ft, and turning to port, dived right onto his tail, opening fire from 300 yards and closing to 150 yards. I fired a four-second burst, seeing strikes and flashes all over the enemy aircraft. The enemy aircraft lost height gradually, with smoke and flames coming from it, skimmed for some distance along the surface of the water and then sank. I orbited around taking ciné gun snaps of the oil patch and pieces of wreckage that were visible.'

The CO was not the only one to enjoy success, as Jean Maridor also destroyed one of the intruders to claim his third victory, as did Davy to claim his second kill. Finally, Johnny Round also made a single victory claim. No 91 Sqn's stunning success had well and truly blooded the Griffon Spitfire in action.

Just as importantly, the fight had been visible to many people in Folkestone – a town that had suffered at the hands of the 'tip and run' raiders. These successes proved something of a tonic to civilian morale in the immediate area. The action had also confirmed the pilots' view that the Spitfire XII was far more effective at low-level than their previous Spitfire Vs had been. Finally, this engagement also drew praise from no less an individual than the Commander-in-Chief of Fighter Command, Sir Trafford Leigh-Mallory, who signalled 'Heartiest congratulations on your fine achievement yesterday. Well done No 91 Sqn'.

Plt Off Davy tangled with an Fw 190 again on 6 June when he and Sgt Waterson witnessed an attack on Eastbourne. They quickly spotted the culprit – an Fw 190A from 7./SKG 10, flying at very low level three miles ahead of them. The Spitfires easily overtook the Focke-Wulf and attacked it together, Waterson eventually delivering the *coup de grace* with a long burst from 100 yards that caused the fighter-bomber to crash into the sea.

Ten days later, one of No 91 Sqn's future stars, Flg Off Ray Nash (who later became very successful in the campaign against the V1s), shot down an Fw 190 over the Channel for his second victory. Shortly after 0600 hrs on the 16th, he and Belgian pilot Flg Off V P Seydel had been scrambled from Hawkinge to escort a Walrus of No 277 Sqn on a rescue mission. Having picked up the downed pilot, the Walrus pilot could not take off again due to the choppiness of the sea. Left with no other option but to taxi the ungainly amphibian all the way back to the Kent coast, the Walrus pilot relied on the the escorting Spitfires to cover him. A short while later they themselves were attacked by a large number of Fw 190s from II./JG 26. Nash claimed one of these destroyed and another was credited to Seydel, although the Belgian was in turn shot down. Despite being wounded, he was soon rescued by an Air-Sea Rescue (ASR) launch.

No 91 Sqn seemed to have the better of these early encounters with JG 26, for on 16 July Sqn Ldr Harries (flying MB831/DL-R) shared in the destruction of an Fw 190 over Poix airfield, near Abbeville. Two days later, again over Poix, Ray Harries became the first pilot to achieve five victories with the Griffon-engined Spitfire when he shot down no fewer than three Fw 190s while flying MB831. These proved to be his last victories with No 91 Sqn, as the following month Harries was promoted to lead the Westhampnett Wing. His replacement at Hawkinge was Sqn Ldr Norman Kynaston, who had been his 'A' Flight commander.

The day that Harries achieved his trio of victories was, conversely, a black one for No 41 Sqn, as Flt Sgt 'Jackie' Fisher was hit by flak and wounded on a sweep and Flg Off Tom Slack was shot down by a Bf 109G. He bailed out and, after many adventures, managed to evade and return via Gibraltar. Sadly, in this same action Flg Off 'Dickie' Hogarth, who had claimed the Griffon Spitfire's first victory in April, was shot down and killed by a Bf 109. The unit also gained a new commanding officer in July with the arrival of Sqn Ldr Bernard Ingham, who had four victories to his name.

ACTION OVER FRANCE

As both defensive and offensive operations continued, so other established aces began achieving success with the Griffon Spitfire. Among them was 22-year-old New Zealander Flt Lt Gray Stenborg of No 91 Sqn, who had previously claimed 11 victories during the Malta battles. On 24 August he had shared in the destruction of an Fw 190 near Beaumont-le-Roger, and a second Focke-Wulf fighter fell to his guns 11 days later. His CO, Sqn Ldr Norman Kynaston (flying MB803/DL-D) also claimed his first victory on 4 September when he downed an Fw 190 over the French coast near Le Touquet. Finally, No 41 Sqn's Flg Off C R 'Jumbo' Birbeck (in EN608) claimed his second victory on this date when he destroyed yet another Fw 190 again near Le Touquet. His kill was also recognised as being No 41 Sqn's 150th victory of the war.

It was, however, No 91 Sqn that seemed to be in the ascendant at this time, as four days later Flt Sgt R A B 'Red' Blumer claimed an Fw 190 near Lille, and the 16th brought the unit yet more success. Led by Sqn Ldr Norman Kynaston in MB803, No 91 Sqn escorted a 'Ramrod' to Beaumont-le-Roger airfield. Close to the target, the unit engaged ten Fw 190s from 4./JG 26, and in the resulting dogfight the squadron CO downed the fighter flown by Unteroffizier Gasser. Kynaston recalled in his Combat Report;

'Just as the Wing Leader reported Fw 190s over his squadron, three Fw 190s flew over my squadron some 1000 ft above us. I swung the unit to port in a climbing turn into the sun and headed for the enemy aircraft, and they immediately turned and began diving away. We overtook them and they split up in various directions.

New Zealander Flg Off Gray Stenborg was already an ace with 12 victories to his credit following his service in Malta with Nos 111 and 185 Sqns by the time he joined No 91 Sqn in 1943. He would go on to claim a further three and one shared victories in the Spitfire XII prior to being killed in action over France on 24 September 1943 (*R C Hay*)

'I saw one on my starboard side and chased him inland, opening fire first of all out of range in the hope that he would turn, and then closing to 300 yards, whereupon I gave him a fairly long burst. I observed strikes on the cockpit and fuselage, and the aircraft, which was at tree-top height, turned slightly to port and flew into the ground, breaking up and catching fire. Then I saw an Fw 190 some distance behind me, and immediately turned and got onto his tail. I gave chase and opened fire at 300 yards, seeing no strikes but observing pieces flying off the aircraft. I then ran out of ammunition and broke off the engagement.'

Among the Free French pilots that flew the Spitfire XII with No 91 Sqn was Flg Off 'Jaco' Andrieux who eventually achieved a wartime total of six destroyed (*P Listemann*)

Also successful was Flt Lt Gray Stenborg, who said of the action after Kynaston had led the squadron down;

'We were left behind in the dive, and when at about 5000 ft an Me 109 flew past me heading inland. I immediately turned 90 degrees right and followed him to ground level – after quite a long chase another Me 109 went past me about 150 yards away in almost the opposite direction. I did a very steep climbing turn – almost a loop – after this one. I fired two short bursts at about 15 degrees angle of attack, observing no hits. He then straightened out and went into a shallow dive. I fired a one- to two-second burst from dead astern at about 200 yards and observed strikes and bits and pieces falling off the fuselage. The Me 109 continued this dive and burst into flames as it hit the ground.'

Free French pilot Flg Off Jaques 'Jaco' Andrieux, flying MB839/DL-V, also shot down a Bf 109G for his first victory in the Spitfire XII and second in total. The cosmopolitan make-up of the squadron was emphasised by the fact that another of the successful pilots was the Australian 'Red' Blumer, who claimed the second of his four victories, as he described in his Combat Report;

'When covering Flt Sgt Bernard Mulcahy RAAF heading back out of France, six Fw 190s attacked us. I broke into them, broke up their attack and got onto one Fw 190's tail. I followed the Fw 190 to the ground, firing at close range and noticing many strikes on the fuselage and bits and pieces flying off the aircraft. The Fw 190 then rolled onto its back and almost immediately struck the ground upside down and exploded. About eight more Fw 190s then bounced me from above. I left the wreckage blazing fiercely, and escaped by violent evasive action until over the French coast, where I lost the enemy.'

Unfortunately, Mulcahy's Spitfire was badly shot up by the German fighters and the Australian bailed out off the coast and became a PoW.

On 19 September Wg Cdr Ray Harries shot down an Fw 190 over Bailleul for his first success as leader of Tangmere Wing, while Flt Lt Chris Doll, who was also on a 'Ramrod', destroyed an Fw 190 near Lille to claim his first Griffon Spitfire victory. However, during the fight with more than 50 enemy fighters Flg Off Geoff Bond was shot down and

One of the aces who made five claims (four of which were destroyed) flying the Spitfire XII was Flt Lt Chris Doll of No 91 Sqn. He also flew the Mk XIV with the unit (*C Doll*)

Flt Lt Don Smith of the RAAF claimed one victory when flying the Spitfire XII while serving as 'A' Flight commander with No 41 Sqn. This success took him to acedom, as he had previously claimed three and one shared kills in July 1942 while flying Spitfire VCs with No 126 Sqn during the defence of Malta (*No 41 Sqn Records*)

killed by *experte* Hauptmann Karl Borris of I./JG 26 and 'Red' Blumer was forced to bail out off Deal, but was picked up by an ASR launch.

Harries was successful once again on the 22nd when he shot down an Fw 190 south of Evreux and probably destroyed a second. Flying with him on the sweep was Australian pilot Flt Lt Don Smith of No 41 Sqn, who destroyed a second Fw 190 for his sole Spitfire XII victory. This success made Smith an ace, nevertheless. Fellow No 41 Sqn pilot Flg Off 'Jumbo' Birbeck claimed an Fw 190 probably destroyed, but on the way home his Spitfire XII's engine failed and he bailed out of EN609 some 20 miles south of Ford. As he weighed over $16^{1}/2$ stones, the squadron records suggest that the 19-year-old pilot would have made a big splash when he landed in the Channel!

The following day Flt Lt Doll, flying MB842/DL-Y, destroyed an Fw 190, and Gray Stenborg downed a Bf 190G near Verneuil for his 15th, and final kill. His Combat Report stated;

'I was flying "Yellow 3" at 13,000 ft when I saw what turned out to be eight Fw 190s diving below the bombers. I immediately dived down and intercepted them coming up dead astern. Two pulled up very steeply, and I led my No 2 after them. On looking behind I saw an Fw 190 coming up onto me. I went into a terribly steep turn to the left, but the Fw 190 seemed quite able to stay behind me. He was firing at 150 yards – I thought "this was it" when all of a sudden I saw an explosion near the cockpit of the Fw 190, upon which it turned onto its back and disappeared from my view.

'I then saw an Me 109 and attacked at about 75 degrees, allowing two rings' deflection. Almost immediately tracer started shooting past me. I broke as hard left as I could and, much to my amazement, saw this Me 109 dead ahead of me. I fired about a four-five second burst at 200-300 yards and saw flashes on the fuselage. A large piece flew off him and he went into a dive upside down (this was at about 1500 ft) pouring white smoke. I saw him hit the ground and blow up. About six more chased me out on the deck.'

It is possible that his very narrow escape may have unsettled Gray Stenborg, for he was killed in action the following day in Spitfire XII MB805 during a head-on attack on an Fw 190 over Poix.

No 41 Sqn was also up on 24 September, and Malta ace Flt Lt Arthur 'Pinky' Glen shot down two Fw 190s near Beauvais – his only Mk XII successes, taking his total to nine destroyed. Flg Off Emmanual Galitzine also claimed an Fw 190, although No 41 Sqn's Flt Lt Hugh Parry was shot down and made a PoW.

Both Spitfire XII squadrons consistently found action over the near Continent during offensive operations in coming weeks, with No 91 Sqn's Free Frenchman 'Jaco' Andrieux continuing on his path to acedom by destroying an Fw 190 (in MB839) on 18 October.

Two days later, Wg Cdr Ray Harries shot down a brace of Bf 109Gs north of Rouen for his last claims with the Griffon Spitfire. Also making his final claim against an aircraft on this date was his successor in No 91 Sqn, Sqn Ldr Norman Kynaston, who downed an Fw 190 to record his fifth success, as did Chris Doll, who destroyed a Bf 109G to 'make ace'. Also successful was Flg Off Ray Nash with a Bf 109G victory in the same area, while Flt Sgt 'Red' Blumer claimed a Bf 109G near Evreux and Flg Off Peter Cowell of No 41 Sqn downed an Fw 190 – the first of his four kills.

October saw another talented and experienced pilot join No 91 Sqn in the shape of the recently commissioned Plt Off Paddy Schade, who had scored 13.5 victories over Malta the previous year. However, 'Red' Blumer, the talented Australian, was downed by flak during a 'Rhubarb' on 6 November, although he evaded capture and returned to the squadron the following June.

ENTER THE Mk XIV

In early January 1944, 'Pinky' Glen became CO of No 41 Sqn, which along with No 91 Sqn continued flying the Spitfire XII. By then the first examples of the next production version of the Griffon-engined Spitfire had also begun to reach Fighter Command. Early-build Mk XIVs had started to roll off the production line in October 1943, and on 4 January 1944, No 610 'County of Chester' Sqn, led by Sqn Ldr Dickie Newbery,

Nine-victory ace Flt Lt 'Pinky' Glen initially served as a flight commander with No 41 Sqn, before subsequently commanding the unit. He claimed his final two victories flying the Spitfire XII when he destroyed a pair of Fw 190s over northern France on 24 September 1943 (*P H T Green Collection*)

No 610 Sqn was the first Spitfire XIV unit, and leading this section of early-build aircraft during the summer of 1944 is the unit CO, and V1 ace, Sqn Ldr Dickie Newbery (*A P Fergusson*)

moved to Exeter and began re-equipping with them. The unit flew the Spitfire XIV's first operational sorties four days later, but things remained fairly quiet as it developed tactics which made the best use of the new type.

During February No 610 Sqn began service trials using 130-octane fuel in an effort to boost the Griffon's performance, but this was found to cause increased lead deposits on the plugs. A further problem arose during routine engine inspections when groundcrew discovered that a significant number of exhaust stubs had cracked, necessitating their immediate replacement. Although these modifications were unsuccessful, others that were introduced did indeed improve the performance and reliability of the Griffon 65.

As more aircraft were delivered, on 28 February No 91 Sqn began exchanging its Spitfire XIIs for XIVs following a move to Castle Camps. A week later, on 7 March, No 610 Sqn gave the aircraft its combat debut when a section comprising Plt Off Hussey and Flt Sgt Harding were patrolling low over the sea south of Start Point, in Devon, under control of Kingswear radar. Late in the afternoon, both pilots were ordered to investigate a contact to the southeast, and after a short time, in poor visibility, they spotted three Fw 190 *'Jabos'* flying at 300 ft. No 610 Sqn's operational record book described this initial encounter;

'Black Section immediately pulled round to the right, and it seemed that the enemy aircraft saw us at the same moment, for as our section turned on their tails, black smoke was seen pouring from their engines as they pushed everything forward and dived to sea level. The Fw 190 on the left of the section turned south, and the other two turned away and disappeared into the haze and glare of the sun. Our section gave chase to the single Fw 190 which, at this time, was about 800 yards ahead right on the deck. We closed without difficulty, but when 400 yards away, "Black 1" noticed an Fw 190 making a quarter attack on him from between "four" and "five o'clock", so gave the order to "break right". As he pulled up, he saw the enemy aircraft firing at him with insufficient deflection, and it appeared that the turning circle of the Spitfire XIV was better than that of the Fw 190.

'"Black 1", at 1000 ft, was now in the haze, and lost sight of the Fw 190 and his No 2'. The pair continued to have brief contact with the enemy trio, and as Harding ('Black 2'), closed fast on the left hand aircraft he 'saw strikes on both wing roots and panels flew off the port mainplane as he closed to about 100 yards. Not until the strikes were observed did the other enemy aircraft take any action. Even then he did nothing for some time, then pulled straight up and round to the left and tried to get on the tail of "Black 2". "Black 2" took a final squirt at his target, whose only evasive action was pitching slightly up and down'.

Although Harding only claimed a 'damaged', the Spitfire XIV had been blooded.

Two days after No 610 Sqn had given the Spitfire XIV its combat debut, Dutch-manned No 322 Sqn, commanded by South African Air Force officer Maj K C Kuhlmann (who had made eight claims, including four destroyed, with No 185 Sqn over Malta in 1942), moved to Acklington, where it too began re-equipping with the potent new fighter. Squadron pilots were impressed with their new mounts, although they expressed their concerns about its modest range and poor cockpit heating.

The aircraft were soon adorned with the Dutch inverted orange triangle marking, and among the first batch delivered, on 14 March, was NH700. This immediately became Keith Kuhlmann's mount, although the fighter did not last long, as on 11 April Flg Off van Hamel suffered a fatal crash in it. Kuhlmann had managed a handful of flights in the aircraft prior to its demise, however, with the first of these taking place on 17 March. He set out his first impressions of the Mk XIV in the unit's diary soon after this sortie;

'Went up to 40,000 ft and did not experience any feeling of being cold or suffering any aftereffects, and no sweater was worn on this trip! Struck by the Griffon engine. The best heights were 12,000 ft and 25,000 ft. IAS at one time was 430 mph, and landing at 110 mph when over the fence. Pilots will have to get used to the different trimming required before any formation flying takes place. A different kind of aircraft!'

The original Griffon-engined unit, No 41 Sqn, was still flying the Mk XII at this point, and on 26 March future four-victory pilot Flg Off Peter Cowell had a near miss when MB882/EB-B bounced off the surface of the water while flying low over the Channel returning from a sweep. He managed to stagger back into the air with shattered propeller blades and limp back to base.

Mk XIV deliveries had been fairly slow up to April 1944, when, at last, No 610 Sqn's diarist noted that 'The Squadron is now fully equipped with Spitfire Mk XIV aircraft'.

On 23 April Keith Kuhlmann's No 322 Sqn began operations following a move to Hartfordbridge when Flg Off G F J Jongbloed and Sgt van Valkenburg scrambled to intercept an unidentified aircraft that turned out to be friendly. This was followed by three more pairs being scrambled, but these too proved uneventful.

No 91 Sqn had also moved back south to West Malling, and on 26 April Flt Lt Chris Doll was scrambled in a Spitfire XIV after a pair of high-flying Fw 190s. Told to climb to 44,000 ft, he eventually engaged

Some of the first Spitfire XIVs delivered in 1944 went to Dutch-manned No 322 Sqn. Amongst its early aircraft was NH700/VL-P seen here, which was delivered on 14 March and assigned to squadron CO, Maj Keith Kuhlmann. The aircraft lasted less than a month, being lost in a fatal accident on 11 April (*Lou Peeters*)

the intruders. During the brief action which ensued, he was wounded and passed out, and he only regained consciousness when passing through 7000 ft. Doll managed to crash-land his Spitfire, although his wounds saw him hospitalised for a number of weeks, thus ending his operational career. Two days later No 91 Sqn's Flg Offs Johnny Johnson and Roy Cruickshank flew the first Mk XIV sortie over the Continent, intercepting a 'bogey' over France which eventually turned out to be a lone USAAF P-38 Lightning! The next day the unit gained the dubious distinction of suffering the first Spitfire XIV loss on operations when Flg Off John Collis failed to return from a patrol over the Thames Estuary.

All three Mk XIV squadrons were active in the weeks prior to the Allied invasion of France, with their primary mission being to keep enemy reconnaissance aircraft away from the landing forces that were assembling along the south coast of England. The units were also escorting bombers that were softening up targets in the Normandy region prior to the landings. Dickie Newbery's No 610 Sqn recorded the first Mk XIV loss over enemy territory on 28 May when Flg Off B T Colgan became a PoW after being downed by flak in RB175 while strafing a train near Lamballe – a second Spitfire XIV was lost attacking another train on 2 June.

On D-Day itself No 41 Sqn was based at Bolt Head, in Devon, and the unit mainly flew 'Roadstead' patrols over the western approaches to the invasion area. No 91 Sqn was at West Malling, and it did not fly on D-Day itself, whilst further west was No 322 Sqn at Hartfordbridge and No 610 Sqn at Harrowbeer. The latter unit escorted Typhoons in attacks on the Channel Islands on 6 June, the fighters being tasked with preventing enemy forces from interfering with the landings. No 610 Sqn

Flying MB882/EB-B, Flt Lt Don Smith leads a gaggle of Spitfire XIIs for the camera on 14 April 1944. In the hands of V1 ace Flt Lt Terry Spencer on 3 September 1944, MB882 claimed the Mk XII's last air-to-air victory (*No 41 Sqn Records*)

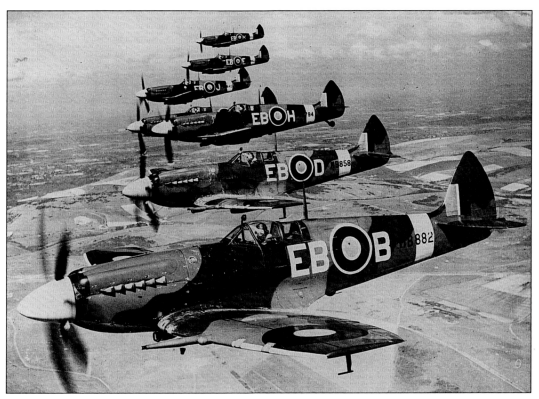

continued to fly such missions in concert with Nos 41 and 263 Sqns throughout the day, while No 322 Sqn finally flew its first sorties during the mid-afternoon when it conducted anti-reconnaissance patrols that continued until dusk.

It was No 41 Sqn that suffered the first Griffon Spitfire loss following the landings when, on 7 June, Flg Off K B Robinson was hit by flak during a 'Roadstead' off Sark and crashed into the sea. That day future star Wt Off Pat Coleman joined the unit, and 24 hours later Wt Off 'Red' Blumer reappeared at No 91 Sqn having finally escaped from France! No 322 Sqn was honoured on the 12th when Queen Wilhelmina and Prince Bernhard visited the unit. That same day a dozen of its pilots escorted USAAF Dakotas towing Waco Hadrian gliders on re-supply sorties to Normandy. Subsequent events would quickly change the focus of Spitfire XIV operations, however.

'DIVER!'

At 0408 hrs on 13 June, the first Fieseler Fi 103 pilotless flying bomb, armed with a 1870-lb warhead, was spotted by the Royal Observer Corps post at Dymchurch. This weapon would quickly become known simply as the V1 (*Vergeltungswaffe* 1 – revenge weapon 1) or 'buzz bomb', but that was officially code-named 'Diver' by the Allies. The launch rate of V1s from sites located in the Pas de Calais quickly increased, and forces to counter this menacing new threat were rapidly deployed.

As well as wide belts of anti-aircraft guns, standing patrols of fighters were maintained off the south coast. Among the squadrons allocated to anti-'Diver' missions were three of the Griffon-engined Spitfire units – No 41 Sqn with its Mk XIIs and Nos 91 and 322 Sqns with their new Mk XIVs, and these were later joined by Nos 130 and 610 Sqns too.

Leaning on the propeller of this No 322 Sqn Spitfire XIV that is wearing recently applied '3W' codes is Flg Off Rudi Burgwal, who with 19 and 5 shared destroyed was the most successful Griffon Spitfire pilot against the V1 flying bomb. Sat on the wing, wearing the hat, is fellow V1 ace Flg Off J Jonker (*Harry van der Meer*)

No 91 Sqn destroyed its first 'Diver' during the morning of the 16th when Flt Lt H B Moffett was scrambled against one coming in over Dungeness. Intercepting the V1 over Tonbridge, he had to chase it for 20 miles before shooting it down near Redhill.

On the 14th, Flt Lt John Draper (a Canadian ace from the North African campaign) joined the squadron, while three days later fellow ace Flt Lt Paddy Schade, flying RB180, made the first of his four 'Diver' claims when he shared in the destruction of a V1 north of Hastings. This was one of three destroyed by the squadron that day.

No 322 Sqn was quickly moved to West Malling to operate alongside No 91 Sqn, their high performance Spitfire XIVs being right in the forefront of the defences against this dangerous new threat. No 322 Sqn opened its account on the 18th, when Flg Offs Meljiers and Burgwal each destroyed one – the first of 110 V1s to be claimed by the unit. Burgwal's Combat Report recorded how the leading anti-V1 Spitfire pilot made the first of his 24 claims. '"Yellow 2" saw a "Diver" travelling inland over Hastings at 1000 ft. Attacked from 600 yards and it exploded'.

Also on the 18th No 91 Sqn's CO, Sqn Ldr Norman Kynaston (in RB185), shot down two V1s – one off Dungeness and the other he chased to bring down near London. By the end of July he had destroyed a further fifteen of his total of 22 V1s destroyed, thus making him one of the leading Griffon Spitfire V1 aces. Also making his first claims against the V1 on 18 June was Ray Nash, who, flying RB169, destroyed one and shared three others. He made his fifth 'Diver' claim a week later, and ended with a total of 20 destroyed, making him the third most successful pilot flying Griffon-engined Spitfires.

Nos 91 and 322 Sqns formed No 24 Wing at this time, which was led by Wg Cdr Bobby Oxspring, a successful ace with 13.5 victories. He said of the V1 campaign;

'We found the ideal tactics for destroying the menacing missiles to be crucially governed by the range at which we fired. Over 250 yards usually hit the flying control system of the craft, which would dive into the ground still with an active warhead. Often a range of 150 yards or less almost always clobbered the warhead, which could severely damage the attacking fighter. The ultimate lay in shooting between 200 and 250 yards, which provided a reasonable certainty of exploding the warhead in the air without undue damage to the fighter. Not surprisingly, the standard of shooting by the squadrons deployed against the "Divers" improved to a very high standard. Our ace on No 24 Wing was the Dutchman Rudi Burgwal of No 322 Sqn who, in a total of 21, demolished five in one sortie.

'The Spitfire XIV's speed was a vital adjunct to the defence requirements against the "Diver" assault on London, and the original plan for No 24 Wing to move to Normandy on D-plus 30 days was shelved.'

On 20 June Harrowbeer-based No 610 Sqn finally got in on the action too. Its CO, Sqn Ldr Dickie Newbery, who had six claims against aircraft (including four destroyed), was patrolling near Tonbridge at lunchtime when he shot down a flying bomb. He later wrote;

'Under "Fairchild" control, I sighted and chased a "Diver" on course 340 degrees, speed 320 mph, at a height of 2500 ft. I opened fire at 250 yards and the jet exploded – its bomb burst upon hitting the ground.'

Sqn Ldr Dickie Newbery had a successful tour as No 610 Sqn's CO, for having previously made nine claims (including three destroyed) flying Spitfires, he became the first Griffon Spitfire V1 ace during the summer of 1944 (*E W Wooten*)

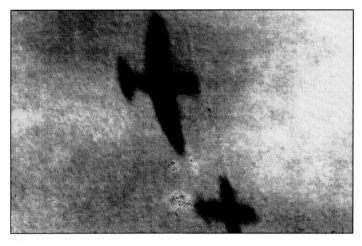

One of the more creative ways used by Spitfire pilots to destroy V1s was to tip them over with their wings – as is about to happen as this Spitfire approaches a flying bomb (*via B Cull*)

That evening he was up again. 'At 2145 hrs, ten miles north west of Bexhill, I fired on another that glided down to explode in a wood'. Also up was Flt Lt John Shepherd, who wrote, 'Opened fire 200 yards, "Diver" exploded in the air. Flew into explosion, without damage to aircraft'. Two days later Newbery bagged another pair, and on the 23rd became the first pilot to claim five of them when he shared in the destruction of another. He was the first of no fewer than 28 Griffon Spitfire pilots to become V1 aces.

Also successful was his opposite number in No 322 Sqn, Maj Keith Kuhlmann, who at 2230 hrs on the 23rd shot down a V1. Earlier that same day, future eight-kill V1 ace Flg Off Maurice Balasse of No 41 Sqn was returning from an anti-'Diver' patrol when he ran out of fuel in MB830/EB-Q and crashed.

23 June had also seen one of No 91 Sqn's Australian pilots, Flg Off Ken Collier in Mk XIV NM698/DL-F, execute a cool act during his 'Diver' patrol. Having taken off from West Malling at 2200 hrs, 50 minutes later, in failing light, he spotted a V1 crossing the coast at 2500 ft and gave chase. The daily Air Defence Great Britain report described the following few minutes;

'"Diver" sighted over Beachy. Strikes seen from bursts fired with no effect. Pilot ran out of ammunition, and being close behind, overtook "Diver", formated alongside it and, with his wing, tipped it over on his second attempt. "Diver" spun in and exploded upon hitting the ground.'

This was the first recorded instance of this manoeuvre, which destabilised the missiles' gyroscopic guidance system. The squadron diary was more descriptive;

'He came across this particular "Diver" just after it had crossed over Beachy, and immediately gave chase. Getting within range, he fired, with no apparent effect as it carried straight on. This peeved him somewhat, so he had another go, and in fact several goes, but still nothing happened, and what was worse he had run clean out of ammo.

'By this time Ken was really swearing mad, and was determined to do or die. He therefore formated with it, and with his wing tipped it over. On his second attempt, down it went in a tight spin, but it very nearly landed in the centre of the town. However, it did no damage, and Flg Off Collier thus brought into practice a new method of getting rid of these flying bombs.'

The first Dutch pilot to successfully complete this delicate manoeuvre, on 27 June, was Flg Off Frans van Eijk of No 322 Sqn (*Lou Peeters*)

This was the second of Ken Collier's seven V1 kills, while with almost 190 claims, No 91 Sqn was the leading anti-'Diver' Griffon Spitfire unit.

Despite these success, the squadron suffered a great loss on the 25th, when Wt Off 'Red' Blumer spun in and was killed soon after taking off on an anti-'Diver' sortie.

On the 28th Flg Off G F J Jongbloed, flying some 20 miles north of Hastings, shared a V1, and within a month he had become a V1 ace with a total score of one aircraft destroyed and one damaged and eight and two shared V1 flying bombs shot down. Later that evening, at 2245 hrs, his CO, Keith Kuhlmann, was successful again whilst flying NH586/VL-G, as he stated in his Combat Report;

'Vectored onto "Diver" over Maidstone. Gave chase and fired three long bursts from dead astern. "Diver" turned over, righted itself and then fell to the ground and exploded on a road or railway line near Eynesford.'

The following day was No 322 Sqn's busiest of the anti-V1 campaign, the unit flying 62 sorties, during which it destroyed ten flying bombs. The pace was maintained the next day when, just inland from Hastings, Rudi Burgwal shot down two to become No 322 Sqn's first V1 ace. On 8 July, whilst patrolling over the coast in the Rye area, he downed no less than five – the most in a single day for any pilot during the campaign against the flying bombs. The next day John Draper caused much consternation to those on the ground by chasing a 'Diver' at low level over West Malling while blazing away with his cannon! He nonetheless claimed his fourth V1, and within a few days had also become a V1 ace.

Another pilot who had recently joined No 610 Sqn was eight-victory Australian ace Flt Lt Tony Gaze, who despite having fought on the Channel front since 1941, regarded anti-V1 work as 'very frightening'. Flying bomb hunting was no sinecure, and was indeed highly dangerous, for on 12 July No 322's Flg Off Maier was killed by an exploding V1 when trying to tip it with his wing.

Eleven days later Flg Off Maurice Balasse of No 41 Sqn shared in the destruction of his fifth V1 to become a 'Diver' ace.

During the spring of 1944, No 91 Sqn converted onto the Spitfire XIV, and during the summer it became heavily involved in the anti-'Diver' campaign. NH654, seen here at Deanland during July, was used by Free French ace Flt Lt Jean-Marie Maridor to achieve a V1 victory on the 5th of that month (*R S Nash*)

However, by this time Allied advances in France, combined with the incessant bombing of suspected launch sites, caused a marked reduction in the number of missiles being launched at London. The strategy for the defences changed too, with both Nos 91 and 322 Sqns moving forward to the advanced landing ground at Deanland to catch the missiles as they neared the coast.

The Dutch squadron reached its V1 'ton' at the end of July when Flt Sgt van Beers brought one down, but the following day (31st), No 91 Sqn suffered a severe blow. Flg Off Paddy Schade, flying RM654, was chasing a V1 in poor visibility when he collided with a Tempest from No 486 Sqn that was closing on the same target. He was killed in the crash. This was followed by the loss of another distinguished No 91 Sqn pilot on 3 August when Flt Lt Jean-Marie Maridor was killed. He had intercepted a V1 over Kent, but it did not immediately crash after being hit and glided towards Benenden School. In an act of cool courage, the Free Frenchman closed to point blank range and opened fire, causing the flying bomb to explode, but destroying his Spitfire in the process. The loss of the two aces was a sad end to No 91 Sqn's anti-V1 campaign, as the unit was withdrawn from the role a few days later.

With Allied armies rapidly capturing many of the areas where the V1 launch sites were located, the intensity of the flying bomb campaign gradually decreased, but they were still launched in sufficient numbers to remain a real threat to London, thus keeping the defenders busy.

On 5 August, for example, No 610 Sqn's Flt Lt Tony Gaze destroyed a V1 that had approached him from behind. Making the most of the Spitfire XIV's agility, he was able to turn quickly and close the range so as to be in a good position to ensure the destruction of the pilotless flying bomb. In spite of many patrols, however, this was his only V1 success. Late in the evening two days later, at around 2300 hrs, No 322 Sqn's Rudi Burgwal claimed his 24th V1 victory (of which five were shared). He described his last success against a flying bomb thus;

'When coming into land, I was told by flying control that a "Diver" was over my base. I gave chase and attacked from line astern at a range of 150 yards. The light went out and the "Diver" went into a glide. I noted a red light warning that I was near a balloon barrage. As I turned for base, I saw the glare from the flying bomb's explosion and felt the blast.'

No 322 Sqn flew its last 'Diver' patrol on 10 August, and during the course of the mission Flg Off Jan Plesman downed the unit's final V1 to take his own total to 11 destroyed. No 322 Sqn had claimed the destruction of 128 V1s, although only 110 were officially credited, and seven of its pilots had become V1 aces. Flg Off Rudi Burgwal was the unit's top scorer (and the most successful Spitfire XIV pilot of the 'Diver' campaign), and he was subsequently lost on 12 August while escorting a Lancaster raid on Orléans.

With anti-V1 operations now tailing off, changes were in the wind for the still quite small Griffon Spitfire force, and on 9 August Nos 91 and 322 Sqns were ordered to deliver their Spitfires XIVs to Nos 350 and 402 Sqns at Hawkinge. Within a few days both units were given a new task – close air support for Allied troops fighting in Europe and long-range fighter escort, for which they were re-equipped with Spitfire IXs. Being issued with the latter was viewed by the pilots as a retrograde step.

Flt Lt Jean-Marie Maridor died in gallant circumstances when claiming his final V1 success on 3 August 1944 over Kent (C H Goss Archive)

Sqn Ldr Mike Donnet made a total of nine claims in Spitfires, although none during his time with No 350 Sqn – they all came in Spitfire V/IXs while serving with No 64 Sqn in 1942-43. A pre-war pilot with the Aviation Militaire Belge, he had made a daring escape from his native Belgium in a Stampe SV 4 biplane in July 1941 (*M L Donnet via D C Hencken*)

Spitfire XIV NM693/MN-S participated in No 350 Sqn's first operation on 10 August 1944. It was regularly flown during that month by unit CO Sqn Ldr Mike Donnet, and later by several other successful pilots, including Sgts Pauwels and Kicq (*via J D R Rawlings*)

Both the 'new' units began operations on 10 August, with the Canadians of No 402 Sqn being led by eight-victory ace Sqn Ldr Wilbert Dodd. The unit started at noon when anti-'Diver' patrols were mounted in the Ashford area of central Kent. One was eventually sighted and attacked by Flt Lt de Niverville, but without success. No 402 Sqn continued these patrols until 25 August, by which time it had destroyed five V1s.

The Belgians of No 350 Sqn flew their first Spitfire XIV sorties at the same time, and their CO, Sqn Ldr Mike Donnet, who had a total of nine claims (including three destroyed) to his credit, later recalled the switch to anti-'Diver' operations;

'We had sufficient speed to catch them, and one of our pilots on one occasion, having exhausted his ammunition without destroying the thing, flew alongside it and, carefully judging his distance, managed to tip its wing, upset its gyroscopic control device and then watch it make a curving dive to earth. After that, tipping them off course became a recognised attack technique, and many were destroyed this way.'

Flg Off Vanderveken shot down the squadron's first flying bomb on 15 August, and the next day Flt Sgt Verbeeck got another.

OFFENSIVE ESCORTS

Meanwhile, on 11 August, having moved into Lympne, No 130 Sqn (led by Sqn Ldr Phil Tripe, who had 3.5 victories) also converted to Spitfire XIVs. Interestingly, amongst its pilots was Flg Off Ulf Christiernsson, who was one of the very few Swedish aviators to serve with the Allies. Coincident with No 130 Sqn's arrival, the Lympne Wing received a

In August 1944 the Spitfire XIV-equipped Lympne Wing came under the command of the most successful New Zealand fighter pilot of the war, Wg Cdr Colin Gray, seen here during his earlier service in Sicily (*C F Gray*)

Belgian ace Flt Lt Alain Plisnier of No 350 Sqn claimed his final success on 19 August 1944, when, flying a Spitfire XIV, he shot down a Ju 188 near Brussels (*A van Haute*)

distinguished new commander when the leading New Zealand ace of World War 2, Wg Cdr Colin Gray, arrived to take over. He later described his thoughts about the Spitfire XIV in his autobiography;

'Nos 130 and 610 Sqns were equipped with Spitfire XIVs, which had the big Griffon 65 engine of 2050 hp and a top speed of 448 mph at 26,000 ft. However, the Spitfire XIV was a high altitude fighter, and barely fast enough at low level to catch a flying bomb, whose speed seemed to vary between 350 and 400 mph. During the next 14 days I spent quite a few hours on anti-"Diver" patrols, but was never once able to fire my guns. There was precious little time to get into a firing pass before the balloon barrage appeared – less than five minutes at the speed we were going.'

From Hawkinge, the pilots of No 350 Sqn also began flying sorties over their homeland, large parts of which had now been liberated. On the 19 August Mike Donnet led a 'Ranger', as he recounted;

'An offensive sweep was planned, and I asked for, and received, permission to fly over Brussels on the way back. I selected 12 pilots, all of whom had homes in the capital. Over the city we flew low in a wide "V" formation along the main boulevards. As I came over the Porte de Namur, I banked steeply and hurled a large Belgian flag from the cockpit which all my pilots had signed. I saw it unfurl in the slipstream and float down, its black, gold and red flapping over the city.'

On the return flight, Flt Lt Alain Plisnier – the 'A' Flight commander, who was flying RM762 – lost contact with the rest of the squadron, and near Soignies came across a Ju 188 that he promptly shot down. His sixth, and final, victory was also No 350 Sqn's only success against a manned aircraft in 1944.

Three days later the Belgians were involved in an action over the now bypassed garrison at Calais, before they conducted several escorts to Boston bombers in attacks around Beauvais. Then, on 28 August, the squadron was formally released from anti-'Diver' operations. Other units too were making their final V1 claims. On 23 August Flt Sgt Geoff Lord of No 130 Sqn shared in the destruction of a flying bomb just south of Dover – his only success against a V1 was also the future ace's first claim of any sort.

Sharing Lympne with No 130 Sqn was No 41 Sqn, which had recently come under the command of Sqn Ldr Douglas Benham (an ace with six victories to his name following his service in North Africa with No 242 Sqn in 1942-43). The unit was still equipped with elderly Spitfire XIIs. That same day Colin Gray suffered an engine failure when taking off in one of them, although he managed to retain control and land safely, as he described;

'I had a narrow squeak when I decided to lead No 41 Sqn on a sweep over the Continent in one of their old Spitfire XIIs. The engine of this machine was very hot, as it had just come down and been refuelled after chasing "buzz bombs", and I found it a bit difficult to start. When it finally did get going it kept cutting on take-off and was so bad that I finally decided to give up. I pulled up a few yards from the far hedge.'

The Canadians in No 402 Sqn were also beginning to go onto the offensive as August came to an end, and on the 26th Sqn Ldr Dodd, flying RM683/AE-N, led a sweep to the Compiegne area during the late

morning. The speedy Spitfires swept over the target at 16,000 ft but nothing was seen, although five of the eleven aircraft returned early with various mechanical troubles. Two days later No 610 Sqn's Flg Off Pat Bangerter, in RM739/DW-O, destroyed two V1s off Dungeness. The following day he shared another, and so became the last Griffon Spitfire pilot to become a V1 ace.

The Lympne Wing also flew some offensive work, as Wg Cdr Gray recalled;

'For the last three days of August we flew three bomber escorts, providing area cover for 240 Bostons bombing Rouen, 100 Halifaxes bombing a "Noball" (V-weapon) target and more Bostons bombing Doullens. However, we did not see a single enemy aircraft.'

His wing, comprising the four Griffon Spitfire squadrons, was now given the primary role of escorting RAF bombers sent to attack targets on the Continent and in western Germany during daylight hours. On the 3 September mission, No 41 Sqn's Plt Off Pat Coleman, flying a Mk XII, shot down the Fw 190 flown by 51-victory *experte* Leutnant Alfred Gross near Tirlemont. The *Staffelkapitan* of 5./JG 26 survived this engagement with wounds, his demise being a significant first scalp for the budding ace, while another future ace, Canadian Flg Off Bill Stowe, sent an Fw 190

As was the privilege of his position, Wg Cdr Colin Gray had his initials applied to the fuselage sides of his personal aircraft, Spitfire XIV RM787, which is seen here at Lympne in September 1944 (*ww2images*)

Also seen at Lympne at the same time was RM797/EB-E of No 41 Sqn, which was the usual mount of future ace Flt Lt Bill Stowe (*W N Stowe via C H Thomas*)

down near Liege for his first success. However, Flt Sgt Peter Chattin was shot down and killed by one of the Focke-Wulfs.

In the same engagement Flt Lt Terry Spencer claimed the Spitfire XII's final victory when he shot down an Fw 190. The V1 ace's only kill was, however, a significant one, as his victim was probably 173 victory *experte* Hauptmann Emil 'Bully' Lang, *Gruppenkommandeur* of II./JG 26.

A week later No 610 Sqn's Spitfire XIVs escorted USAAF B-26s sent to bomb enemy forces trapped against the coast to the north of Ostend, although the only opposition they encountered took the form of unpleasantly accurate light flak. The following day No 350 Sqn crossed into Germany for the first time when escorting bombers to the Ruhr, and on 13 September anti-V2 rocket patrols near the Hague were flown, although, not surprisingly, they proved to be unsuccessful.

On the 17th the Lympne Wing's Spitfires provided escort for the airborne landings at Arnhem, protecting Dakota and Stirling transports performing the initial drop. The fighters also escorted the subsequent re-supply drops, but the Spitfires saw little sign of the Luftwaffe. These sorties continued throughout the period of the epic battle, with No 130 Sqn venturing into Germany for the first time on the 23rd. During this mission Wg Cdr Gray sighted his first German jet, although he was unable to engage it.

With the appearance of Luftwaffe jets over the battlefield, and the need to return the longer-range Mustangs back to Britain for escort operations, Fighter Command decided to gradually move the Spitfire XIV units to join the 2nd TAF on the Continent. Nos 130 and 402 Sqns were the first to move, settling in at B70 Deurne, near Antwerp, as part of No 125 Wing on 30 September.

Back at Lympne, No 41 had at last been re-equipped with Spitfire XIVs, and with Nos 350 and 610 Sqns, continued escort operations from there through the autumn due to a shortage of suitable airfields to accommodate them in Belgium. Typical of the sorties flown during the wing's final weeks in the UK was the mission undertaken on 30 November, when No 610 Sqn's Spitfires escorted 60 Lancasters sent to strike oil targets on the Ruhr. Again, the only opposition seen was flak.

No 41 Sqn's final Spitfire XII accident occurred when Wt Off Weeds crash-landed MB862/EB-E on 11 September 1944. The forlorn looking fighter is seen here being examined by its regular pilot (at right), a somewhat rueful Flt Lt Bill Stowe (*W N Stowe via C H Thomas*)

TO THE RHINE

The deployment of the first Spitfire XIV squadrons to the Continent meant that there was now a much greater opportunity for pilots assigned to these units to engage the remaining Luftwaffe fighter force. Shortly before these units left England, 14-victory ace Wg Cdr Alan Wright, who commanded the Air Fighting Development Unit, had issued Report No 117. This document provided comparative performance figures for the Spitfire XIV when flown against a captured Fw 190 fitted with a BMW 801D engine, and the report was to be a source of some confidence to those pilots that read it;

'The Spitfire XIV should use its remarkable maximum climb and turning circle against any enemy aircraft. In the attack, it can afford to "mix it", but should beware of the Fw 190's quick roll and dive.'

After the trial against the Bf 109G, the report stated bluntly 'The Spitfire XIV is superior to the Bf 109G in every respect'. Wg Cdr Wright's report ended with the comforting conclusions that 'The Spitfire XIV is superior to the Spitfire IX in all respects. It has the best all-round performance of any present day fighter, apart from range'.

Having flown into Antwerp on 10 September, the following day No 130 and 402 Sqns moved over to B82 Grave to join No 125 Wing, which was part of No 83 Group. From here the wing began flying armed reconnaissance and anti-Me 262 fighter patrols over the Nijmegen-Arnhem area. Its wing leader was 15-victory ace Wg Cdr Geoffrey Page, although his spell on the Continent was not to last long, for in the early evening of 5 October he was forced to crash-land RM763 at Grave after being hit by flak near Apeldoorn. Fracturing a bone in his back, Page's long and distinguished operational career was brought to an end. He was replaced by another distinguished ace, Canadian Wg Cdr George Keefer, who had eight victories to his credit from combat tours in North Africa and on the Channel Coast. He would enjoy more success with the Spitfire XIV in coming months.

The nearest Spitfire XIV in this line-up of No 130 Sqn aircraft at B82 Grave in October 1944 is RM655/AP-S, which was flown by future ace Flg Off Geoff Lord when he destroyed enemy vehicles during an armed reconnaissance near Wesel on the 7th of that month. Behind it, *sans* unit codes, sits RM675, which was one of a number of Spitfire XIVs flown at the time by Sgt Freddie Edwards and Flt Lt Marty Hume (*via C F Shores*)

Although the airborne assault on Holland had only been partially successful due to stubborn enemy resistance, the Anglo-Canadian 21st Army Group had isolated enemy garrisons in northern and western Holland and was now in a position to assault the formidable defences of the Siegfried Line along the German border. The broad expanses of the Rivers Maas and Rhine also provided difficult natural obstacles to the advance too, as did the worst autumnal weather seen for many years.

On 6 October No 125 Wing's Spitfires had their first encounter with the enemy since arriving on the Continent when No 402 Sqn flew a sweep in the area from Venlo to Wesel. As the unit neared Nijmegen, more than a dozen Bf 109s attacked them and two were promptly shot down by Flt Lt J B Lawrence and Flg Off Whittaker, the former recording;

'I sighted one '109 alone, crossing in front of me. I turned into line astern and closed quickly. I fired one very short burst and the '109 went into a diving turn to starboard. I turned inside him, and at about 20 degrees off, 200 yards range, I fired another burst of about two seconds. Strikes were observed on the cockpit and engine. Pieces flew off and white and black smoke poured out. The enemy aircraft turned into a steep spiral to port. He hit the ground two or three miles south of Nijmegen.'

Soon afterwards, a pair of Fw 190s was spotted near Millingen, one of which was shot down by Flt Lt Speare, followed a short while later by a lone Bf 109 whose demise was shared by so many pilots that it was claimed for the squadron. This victory completed a hugely satisfactory debut for No 402 Sqn on the Continent.

The enemy's light flak, often cunningly camouflaged, was always a deadly foe during the numerous low-level missions flown by No 125 Wing, and it was responsible for a steady stream of damage, and losses, endured by the Spitfire XIV squadrons. The wing's airfield also suffered occasional attacks from the enemy too, such as on 21 October, when an

In late 1944, two fighter-reconnaissance squadrons received the Spitfire XIV. RM818/C belonged to No 430 Sqn, and the aircraft was subsequently shot down by flak on the last day of 1944, resulting in the loss of Flg Off J N McLeod (via C H Thomas)

Me 262 hit co-located No 127 Wing's side of the base, damaging 18 aircraft. Grave was virtually unusable by then in any case due to the incessant heavy rain, with No 402 Sqn losing two aircraft in an accident in the mud. On 1 November, both of the wing's Spitfire XIV squadrons were forced to move south to B64 Deist (a pre war Belgian airfield).

A few days earlier, on 25 October, Sqn Ldr Wilbert Dodd became tour-expired. He had flown many sorties over the Arnhem-Nijmegen region throughout the autumn, and he flew his final mission on this date over this area in RM651. Back in England, fellow CO Sqn Ldr Mike Donnet had also been promoted, thus bringing to an end his time with No 350 Sqn.

RECCE SPITFIRES

The next Spitfire XIVs to join 2nd TAF were not assigned the fighter role, as during November No 430 Sqn of No 35 Wing, based at B78 Eindhoven, replaced its Mustang Is with camera-equipped FR XIVs. These aircraft were to perform fighter-reconnaissance and artillery spotting missions in direct support of the land battle, the Griffon Spitfire's performance greatly reducing their vulnerability to enemy fighters. Indeed, a significant number of the latter were to be claimed by pilots assigned to the reconnaissance squadron in coming months.

No 430 Sqn's re-equipment, and that of No 2 Sqn, was timely, as on 6 November a dangerous new opponent had made its appearance in the elegant shape of the Jumo 210-powered Fw 190D-9, known to the enemy as the 'Langnasen Dora'. Kept exclusively for the defence of Me 262 bases until now, the 'Dora-9s' of veteran III./JG 54 soon began to make their presence felt, especially as the weather improved for a brief period mid-month.

The rain, fog and low cloud of late autumn soon returned, however, and welcomed the arrival of the three remaining Spitfire XIV units from Lympne when No 41 Sqn went to Deist and Nos 350 and 610 Sqns arrived at B56 Evere, on the outskirts of Brussels, to briefly join No 127 Wing in early December. They had all concentrated within No 125 Wing at Y32 Openhoven by the end of the month, however, with No 402 Sqn joining all-Canadian No 126 Wing at B88 Heesch, where it operated alongside the wing's Spitfire IX units.

On the ground, Allied troops were enduring a gruelling time as they struggled to prevail against a determined and well dug in enemy that was stalling their push towards the Rhine and Germany proper.

8 December saw 2nd TAF units perform several sweeps in mid-afternoon, with No 130 Sqn sending ten Spitfires on an armed reconnaissance led by Wg Cdr George Keefer against 'targets of opportunity' in the Dulmen-Munster area. During a strafing attack, they were engaged

The ebullient Australian Plt Off Freddie Edwards served with No 130 Sqn from the summer of 1944 through to the end of the war, seeing much action and eventually achieving six victories in April-May 1945 (*via C F Shores*)

by a dozen fighters, and in the resulting combat over Burgstein an Fw 190 fell to Flg Off Lowe, whilst Flg Off Riley and Flt Lt Harry Walmsley each claimed a Bf 109. The latter described the third of his 12 victories thus;

'We saw a locomotive with about ten trucks. We had made one attack on the loco and two on the trucks, and were preparing to make another when a dozen aircraft appeared from the east and dived straight past us as if they were joining in the attack on the train! I then saw the crosses on the wings and I could see that they were Me 109s and Fw 190s. A dogfight started, with everyone milling round.

'After about five minutes I found myself alone. I saw another train pulled up in a station, so I went down and had a squirt at it and saw strikes on the locomotive. When I pulled up, I saw a Spitfire in trouble. It was smoking and the undercarriage partly down. I joined up with it to protect it, as did five other Spitfires. I do not know what happened to the damaged Spitfire, for suddenly six enemy aircraft – probably some of the ones I had first seen – came diving down out of cloud. They had obviously climbed and reformed after the initial attack.

'This second attack, made from ten-tenths cloud at 1500 ft, was obviously directed against the damaged Spitfire. Some of the others in the squadron chased them off. I went for two which were making an attack. I made a quarter attack on one of them – an Me 109 – closing to 300 yards and giving it a two-second burst with all guns. I saw strikes behind the cockpit and the enemy aircraft dived straight into the ground. I found I was being fired at by two other enemy aircraft, so I used full evasive tactics for about five minutes and finally got away into cloud.'

The future ace also went on to comment of his opponents;

'I have never seen Huns fight so well. Their tactics were good in that obviously after the first attack they climbed into cloud and reformed. They definitely caught us by surprise. I think they had either been on patrol, or had been scrambled, and when they saw smoke from the train they knew where we were and attacked out of cloud. The Spitfire XIV is definitely better than the Me 109, as I could do a better climbing turn even with my drop tank still on.'

No 130 Sqn's Flt Lt D J Wilson was killed, however.

Two of the newly-arrived squadrons – Nos 41 and 350 Sqns – flew their first sorties that same day, and No 41's patrol spotted some Me 262s that they could not engage. The other new *(text continues on page 41)*

Like Spitfire XIV RM655/AP-S seen on page 29, RM619/AP-D was also photographed at Grave soon after No 130 Sqn's move to the Continent. Later transferred to No 350 Sqn, RM619 subsequently fell victim to flak near Aachen on 16 January 1945. Its pilot, Flt Lt H J Smets, spent the rest of the war as a PoW (*via C F Shores*)

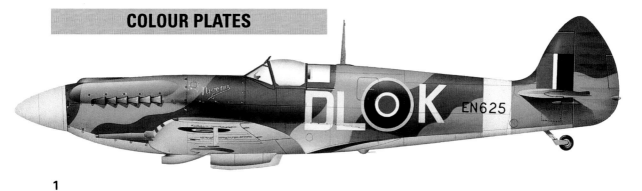

1
Spitfire XII EN625/DL-K of Sqn Ldr R H Harries, No 91 Sqn, Hawkinge, 25 May 1943

2
Spitfire XII EN620/DL-M of Flt Lt G Stenborg, No 91 Sqn, Westhampnett, 23 September 1943

3
Spitfire XII MB839/DL-V of Lt J Andrieux, No 91 Sqn, Westhampnett and Tangmere, September-November 1943

4
Spitfire XIV NH700/VL-P of Maj K C Kuhlmann, No 322 (Dutch) Sqn, Acklington, March 1944

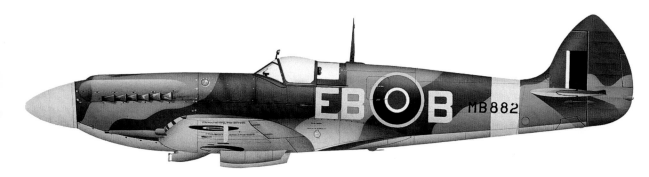

5
Spitfire XII MB882/EB-B of Flt Lt D S Smith, No 41 Sqn, Friston, April 1944

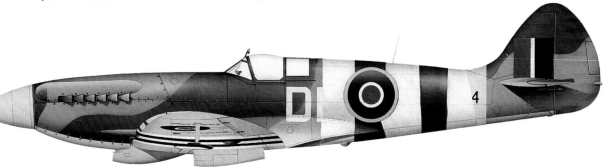

6
Spitfire XIV NH654/DL-? of Flt Lt J-M Maridor, No 91 Sqn, West Malling, 5 July 1944

7
Spitfire XIV RB188/DL-K of Flt Lt H D Johnson, No 91 Sqn, West Malling, July 1944

8
Spitfire XIV RM693/MN-S of Sqn Ldr M L D Donnet, No 350 (Belgian) Sqn, Hawkinge, August 1944

9
Spitfire XIV RM683/AE-N of Sqn Ldr W G Dodd, No 402 Sqn RCAF, Hawkinge, 26 August 1944

10
Spitfire XII MB862/EB-E of Flt Lt W N Stowe, No 41 Sqn, Lympne, September 1944

11
Spitfire XIV RB159/DW-D of Sqn Ldr R A Newbery, No 610 'County of Chester' Sqn, Lympne, September 1944

12
Spitfire XIV RM655/AP-S of Plt Off G Lord, No 130 Sqn, B82 Grave, Holland, October 1944

13
Spitfire XIV RM787/CG of Wg Cdr C Gray, Lympne Wing, Lympne, October 1944

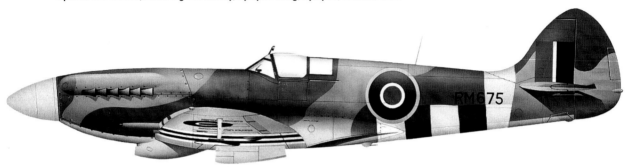

14
Spitfire XIV RM675 of Wt Off F E F Edwards, No 130 Sqn, B82 Grave, Holland, 3 October 1944

15
Spitfire XIV RM862/AE-K of Sqn Ldr L A Moore, No 402 Sqn RCAF, B88 Heesch, Holland, 28 February 1945

16
Spitfire XIV NH745/EB-V of Sqn Ldr D I Benham, No 41 Sqn, B78 Eindhoven, Holland, March-April 1945

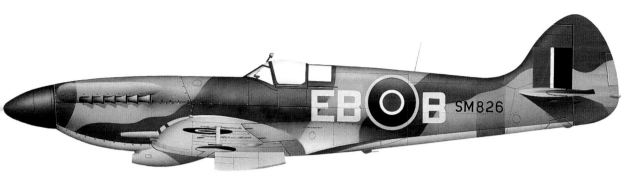

17
Spitfire XIV SM826/EB-B of Sqn Ldr J B Shepherd, No 41 Sqn, B106 Twente, Holland, 14 April 1945

18
Spitfire XIV MV260/EB-P of Flt Lt P Cowell, No 41 Sqn, B118 Celle, Germany, April 1945

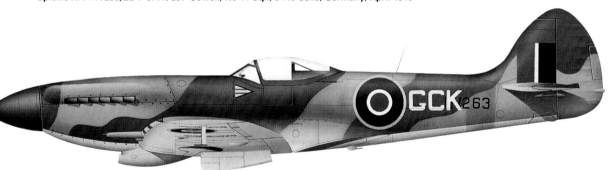

19
Spitfire XIV MV263/GCK of Wg Cdr G C Keefer, No 125 Wing, B106 Twente, Holland,
and B118 Celle, Germany, April 1945

20
Spitfire XIV RB155/MN-C of Plt Off D J Watkins, No 350 (Belgian) Sqn, B118 Celle, Germany, 20 April 1945

21
Spitfire XIV RM931/EB-U of Flt Lt J F Wilkinson, No 41 Sqn, B118 Celle, Germany, 20 April 1945

22
Spitfire XXI LA223/DL-Y of Flt Lt J W P Draper, No 91 Sqn, Ludham, April 1945

23
Spitfire XIV NH689/MN-B of Flt Sgt G F Gigot, No 350 (Belgian) Sqn, B118 Celle, Germany, 30 April 1945

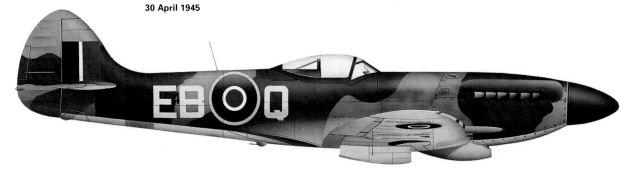

24
Spitfire XIV MV264/EB-Q of Flg Off E Gray, No 41 Sqn, B118 Celle, Germany, 1 May 1945

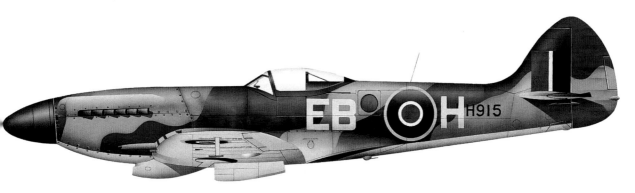

25
Spitfire FR XIV NH915/EB-H of Flt Lt D S V Rake, No 41 Sqn, B118 Celle, Germany, 3 May 1945

26
Spitfire FR XIV NH903/VC-P of Sqn Ldr J B Prendergast, No 414 Sqn RCAF, B156 Luneburg, Germany, May 1945

27
Spitfire XIV MV257/JEJ of Gp Capt J E Johnson, No 125 Wing, Kastrup, Denmark, June 1945

28
Spitfire XIV RN135/YB-A of Sqn Ldr J H Lacey, No 17 Sqn, Seletar, Singapore, September-December 1945

29
Spitfire XIV MV263/JEFF of Wg Cdr G W Northcott, No 126 Wing, B174 Utersen, Germany,
September 1945-March 1946

30
Spitfire XIV RN133/FF-B of Sqn Ldr K L Charney, No 132 Sqn, Kai Tak, Hong Kong, February 1946

31
Spitfire FR 18 TZ203/RG-J of Sqn Ldr C F Ambrose, No 208 Sqn, Ein Shemer, Palestine, September 1947

32
Spitfire FR 18 NH850/Z of Sqn Ldr W G G Duncan-Smith, No 60 Sqn, Kuala Lumpur, Malaya, 31 December 1950

unit, No 610 Sqn, also suffered its first loss to flak when NH719 was downed near Munster on 10 December. Its pilot, Flg Off W A Nicholls, was captured.

The Luftwaffe's renewed aggression during this period may have been an attempt to cover the build up to a huge offensive that opened in the Ardennes at dawn on the 16th under the cover of foul weather. Dubbed the 'Battle of the Bulge', the attack was aimed mainly at the US 1st Army on the British right flank, but the potential threat to the British rear was also serious. Allied air superiority clearly had a key role to play in repelling this offensive, and in spite of the weather, many sorties were flown in an attempt to blunt the thrust. All Spitfire squadrons suffered losses, with Flt Lt Harry Walmsley having to bail out near Liege after being hit by flak on the 22nd, for example.

There was also another threat – namely the US forces that had a tendency to shoot at anything not bearing American 'stars and bars'! No 610 Sqn's Flt Lt Tony Gaze made several notes in his log book about being 'shot at by Mustangs' and 'shot at by Yank flak'. The weather continued to dominate, although it improved markedly on Christmas Eve as a persistent weather depression moved in. The Wing diarist noted;

'The weather is magnificent, the sun shining through the sharp crisp atmosphere. The mush has gone, a hard frost having fixed the water and slush.'

Thus, with US resistance at Bastogne upsetting enemy plans, Allied air power now began to hit bogged down German armoured formations. No 125 Wing also had patrols out, although No 350 Sqn's CO (Sqn Ldr L Collignon) was downed by flak and injured near Malmedy. Luftwaffe fighters were active too, but the wing had no luck. This changed on Christmas Day afternoon when No 402 Sqn's Flg Off Sherk claimed an Fw 190 near Aachen. The enemy rear areas were also pounded, with No 610 Sqn escorting a Lancaster attack on Rheydt on 27 December.

The wing moved to Openhoven at month-end, and during a sweep from its new base on 31 December, No 610 Sqn was attacked once again by US fighters. The Spitfire XIV's stunning climb performance enabled them to easily disengage from the P-51s, however. At dawn the following morning, the Luftwaffe launched Operation *Bodenplatte* – the massive dawn attack on Allied air bases in Belgium and Holland – in the hope of catching RAF and USAAF aircraft on the ground. The enemy aspirations were not to be fulfilled, however, as fighter aircraft were already airborne, and they engaged the inbound enemy.

One of the first combats to be fought was between a Spitfire XIV of No 2 Sqn, flown by Flt Lt Packwood, and a group of Messerschmitt fighters from I./JG 27. The RAF pilot shot down Unteroffizier Braun, flying Bf 109K-4 wk-nr 331344, near Utrecht, as he described in his Combat Report;

'I attacked an Me 109 from dead astern and above – it took no evasive action. I gave it a five-second burst with cannon and machine guns, closing from 400 yards to 150 yards. I observed strikes on the cockpit and fuselage. The aircraft disintegrated, its starboard wing breaking off and the fighter flicking over onto its back and hitting the ground in flames.'

JG 11, however, caught much of No 125 Wing on the ground at Openhoven, as the wing diarist described;

'New Year's Day saw everyone up bright and early, and No 41 Sqn were away on an Armed Recce when the Hun turned up in force and proceeded to strafe us and the American strip nearby. Considering everything, his shooting was poor. No 350 Sqn came off worse, having had seven aircraft unserviceable, but not all badly damaged. No 130 Sqn had one damaged. Two airmen were wounded and a petrol dump set on fire.'

The attacks saw many acts of raw courage by those caught on the ground, amongst them one of No 130 Sqn's future stars, Flt Sgt Phil Clay, who helped direct fire-fighting operations. He was decorated with the British Empire Medal for his actions. Clay subsequently received a DFC and bar during flying operations, thus completing a most unusual combination.

That same morning, No 610 Sqn's Flt Lt Tony Gaze, flying DW-S, shot down an Fw 190D that was almost certainly being flown by 12./JG 2 *Staffelkapitan* Lt Fritz Swoboda. Having claimed his ninth victory, though first on the Mk XIV, the Australian was then attacked by P-51s in the Malmedy area! His was the wing's only victory that morning.

BATTLE THROUGH THE REICHWALD

In spite of the enemy's best efforts, Allied tactical aircraft were soon back in the air, their losses replenished. Not so for the Luftwaffe, which had suffered heavy attrition during *Bodenplatte*, particularly amongst its irreplaceable fighter leaders.

On 4 January 1945 No 350 Sqn finally received a new CO when V1 ace Sqn Ldr Terry Spencer moved over from No 41 Sqn following his promotion. Within days of taking command, his unit's losses had been made good and it continued to send out offensive sorties alongside the other units in the wing as the British and Canadian Divisions prepared for the push through the Reichwald forest to the banks of the Rhine.

The far ranging Spitfire XIVs took a steady toll of enemy transport during this period. For example, on the 14th No 350 Sqn destroyed or damaged 25 vehicles, by which time the so-called 'Battle of the Bulge' had ended. It was not until 23 January that the Spitfire XIV squadrons met the Luftwaffe again when, soon after 0830 hrs, eight fighters from No 41 Sqn (led by the CO, Sqn Ldr Douglas Benham, in RM791/EB-V) spotted some 'Dora-9s' of I./JG 26 at low-level near Munster.

In the unit's first major engagement with the Mk XIV, Benham claimed his final two victories. Having downed one Fw 190D-9, he pulled up to evade fire from a second, having already been struck in the starboard wing. However, when trying to emulate this manoeuvre, the German fighter crashed! A third Focke-Wulf was claimed by Flg Off F M Hegarty for his first victory, as described by his Combat Report;

Seen shortly before No 350 Sqn's move to the Continent, Spitfire XIV RM764/MN-M retained the type E wing, and was later transferred to the post-war Belgian Air Force (*via C H Thomas*)

'After witnessing the squadron CO's combats, I was chased by an Fw 190 and broke very sharply to port, so that I was able to see the Fw 190 trying to follow my manoeuvre, which he failed to do and flicked out of his turn and went straight into the ground from 500 ft. Wt Off P H Hale confirms the destruction of this aircraft, seeing it go up in flames.'

Another Focke-Wulf was damaged by future ace Flt Lt Bill Stowe, who made his first claim on the type. Sadly, however, during the engagement V1 ace Flt Lt Maurice Balasse was shot down and killed, apparently by Feldwebel Hegener in an Fw 190D-9 from III./JG 54. The other units were also out during the day, losing three aircraft to flak, including that flown by Wg Cdr Keefer, who force-landed near Liege.

Within a few days Nos 130, 350 and 610 Sqns moved north to B78 Eindhoven, while No 41 Sqn joined No 122 Wing at B80 Volkel for six weeks. Canadian No 126 Wing, which contained No 402 Sqn, gained another experienced leader in the shape of Wg Cdr Geoff Northcott who replaced fellow ace Wg Cdr Dal Russel at the end of January.

All five of the Griffon Spitfire fighter squadrons, plus the two reconnaissance units continued to generate large numbers of offensive sorties over the northwest German plain, No 610 Sqn's Flt Lt Tony Gaze recording in his log book on 6 February that he flew his regular mount 'DW-T' 'over the snow-bound landscape'.

By this stage the territory lost during the Ardennes offensive had been recovered, with the British and Canadian Armies facing the enemy from Nijmegen, along the German border around Kleve, through the German town of Goch and down toward Roermond, on the Dutch/German border. The priority for Montgomery's 21st Army Group was to clear the Reichwald forest

Parked at Lympne, in rural Kent, in the early autumn of 1944 is Spitfire XIV RM791/EB-V, which was the aircraft that No 41 Sqn CO, Sqn Ldr Douglas Benham, used to shoot down two Fw 190s on 23 January 1945. Flt Lt Frank Woolley was also flying RM791 when he claimed his first Mk XIV success – a probable Fw 190D-9 – on 14 February (*D I Benham via C H Thomas*)

In early 1945 No 350 Sqn was based at Y32 Openhoven, where Spitfire XIV NH689/MN-B was photographed. Despite being the aircraft of squadron CO, Sqn Ldr Terry Spencer, it was flown by a plethora of other successful pilots including Flt Sgts A Kicq and G F Gigot, Flt Lt Frank Woolley and future ace Plt Off Des Watkins (*via C H Thomas*)

ahead of Goch and Kleve, through which passed the northern parts of the West Wall, or Siegfried Line. In an effort to hinder their progress even further, the enemy had allowed large areas of land between the Maas and Rhine to flood.

The assault, named Operation *Veritable*, began on 8 February, with the first success in the air being claimed by a Spitfire XIV of No 402 Sqn flown by Flt Lt Sleep, who, near Coesfeld, shot down a Ju 88 nightfighter flown by the *Kommodore* of NJG 2, 46-victory *experte* Maj Paul Semrau. In spite of heavy resistance, Kleve fell the next day, but further flooding slowed the advance signifi-

cantly. The Griffon Spitfire units, like others, ranged far behind the frontline, interdicting enemy forces – particularly road and rail transport. No 2 Sqn had a successful engagement against a Bf 109 on the 10th during one of these missions. Losses to flak, however, remained steady. On the 13th, a section from No 41 Sqn shot down a Bf 110 nightfighter from 11./NJG 1 near Lippstadt, but the unit gained an even greater success the following day.

On the morning of the 14th, seven of No 41 Sqn's Spitfire XIVs headed for Rheine airfield, where Fw 190s of I./JG 26 and III./JG 54 were covering the launch of Me 262s. As the RAF pilots neared the base at 0830 hrs, they soon spotted a dozen Fw 190Ds circling above several jets that were in the circuit. The Spitfires attacked immediately and hit a number of the enemy fighters. Flt Lt Frank Woolley (who was to end the war with six claims, including four destroyed), in RM791/EB-V, probably destroyed one of the 'Dora-9s', while Wt Off Moyle shot another one down. Then, diving through the covering Focke-Wulfs, Flg Off Eric Gray and Wt Off Rossow each damaged a jet.

The Rheine-based jets of KG(J) 51 were active throughout the day, and shortly before dusk No 610 Sqn's Flt Lt Tony Gaze went one better, as he recalled afterwards in his Combat Report;

'I was leading "Wavey Black" section of two aircraft on a standing patrol over Nijmegen. At about 1630 hrs I sighted an Arado 234 pulling up from attacking the Cleve area. I dropped my tank and attempted to intercept, but despite the fact that I cut the corner, it pulled away easily at 7000 ft. After this, we continually chased Arados over this area. I fired at two without result.

'At about 1700 hrs when it was apparent that the jets were diving down through the cloud, which was from 9000-11,000 ft, I climbed up through it, leaving "Black 2" below, hoping to warn him when they dived. Then I did an orbit at 13,000 ft to clear off the ice on the windscreen and sighted three Me 262s in Vic formation passing below me at cloud-top level.

'I dived down behind them and closed in, crossing behind the formation and attacked the port aircraft, which was lagging slightly.

Although acedom just eluded him, Frank Woolley was a highly distinguished pilot on the Spitfire XIV. He made five claims – four destroyed and a probable – with Nos 41, 350 and 130 Sqns, the latter two of which he commanded. The son of a decorated Sopwith Dolphin pilot from the Great War, Woolley had initially seen action in May 1941 flying Vickers Vincent army co-operation biplanes during the Iraqi Revolt. Remaining in the RAF post-war, and rising to the rank of wing commander, Woolley was killed on 28 November 1959 when his Canberra B 2 crashed near Strubby (*via M Goodman*)

I could not see my sight properly as we were flying straight into the sun, but I fired from dead astern at a range of 350 yards, hitting it in the starboard jet with the second burst, at which the other two aircraft immediately dived into cloud. It pulled up slowly and turned to starboard, and I fired obtaining more strikes on fuselage and jet, which caught fire. The enemy rolled over onto its back and dived through cloud. I turned 180 degrees and dived after it, calling on the R/T to warn my No 2. On breaking cloud I saw an aircraft hit the ground and explode about a mile ahead of me.'

Gaze's tenth victory was Me 262A 9K+NL of 3./KG 51, flown by Feldwebel Rudolf Hoffmann, who was killed. The first jet destroyed by No 125 Wing, it was, however, the 132nd, and last, victory recorded by No 610 Sqn, as a week later the unit withdrew to Warmwell for a period of armament training, only to be disbanded there on 3 March. A number of its pilots, including Tony Gaze, returned to action with other units.

A few days after Nos 41 and 610 Sqn's successes, it was No 350 Sqn's turn, when three of its pilots found 20 Bf 109s near Rheine. Flt Lt Lavigne and Flg Off Lambrechts each destroyed one, the former writing;

'We had chased several Me 262s, which were all heading northeast towards the aerodromes at Rheine and Hopsten, so I decided to re-form the squadron and orbit these aerodromes. I saw two Me 262s going in to land. I was preparing to attack them when I saw three aircraft below me at between nought and 500 ft. I went down and picked out No 2 in the gaggle. The pilot of the enemy aircraft saw me and broke left. I followed him in his turn, and allowing about one-and-a-half rings deflection, I opened fire with all armament from 200 yards, closing to 100 yards, finishing up dead astern of the enemy aircraft. I saw a big explosion in the right wing root and the enemy aircraft, which was then at 500 ft, flicked over on its back and slowed up. It was smoking badly and crashed in the circuit south of the aerodrome.'

For the Belgian unit which had had such a lean time during 1944, it was a great tonic – and the portent of greater things to come.

The following day, 22 February, the Allied air forces launched Operation *Clarion* – a 24-hour-long all out assault on the enemy transport system from railways to canal locks. All the Spitfire XIV units were active, No 41 Sqn losing one aircraft to flak while Nos 130 and 350 Sqns combined on a sweep. No 402 Sqn's operations record book also recorded more domestic information for this date, however;

'It was learned today that Sqn Ldr L A Moore is being posted to the squadron as OC. This is indeed a fortunate move for the squadron, as Sqn Ldr Moore is an experienced pilot, having completed a part of his first tour here.'

In fact Leslie Moore had claimed 1.5 destroyed, a probable and two damaged during this tour, which took place between January 1943 and March 1944, and he now had three and three shared victories to his

One of the aircraft flown by Frank Woolley whilst serving with No 130 Sqn was 'AP-T', seen here taxiing in at B78 Eindhoven in January 1945. He scored three victories in this aircraft (*D S V Rake*)

name following subsequent successes with No 441 Sqn. Two days later, on 24 February, Sqn Ldr Moore flew his first operation of his tour when, in RM906, he led a fighter-bomber attack to the Emmerich-Wesel area. Then, at lunchtime, in RM727/AE-P, Moore led an armed reconnaissance from Volkel, while on the 27th, in RN119/AE-J, he patrolled the Nijmegen-Venlo area, and the following day flew RM862/AE-K on an armed reconnaissance to Munster. That day (28 February), following the capture of Sqn Ldr Terry Spencer 48 hours earlier, Sqn Ldr Frank Woolley from No 130 Sqn was promoted to lead No 350 Sqn. Sqn Ldr Spencer later recalled his relatively brief tenure;

'I joined No 350 "Belgian" Sqn as their CO on 4 January 1945. On 26 February, whilst on a "Rhubarb" in the Rheine area, I was shot down by flak. I called Roberto Muls, my No 2, and advised him that I was on fire. I climbed to 8000 ft and took to my parachute, but hit the tailplane whilst bailing out. When I landed, I was taken prisoner and, fortunately, a lot of French slave workers were around to save me being torn apart.'

After much hard fighting both on the ground and in the air, and in the face of desperate resistance and often appalling weather, the Allies had reached the Rhine by the end of February. Preparations for its crossing, intended to take place at Wesel in late March, were immediately begun.

Early on 2 March a pair of No 41 Sqn Spitfires were scrambled from Volkel, and Australian Flt Lt Dan Reid claimed his second (and final) victory. It was a significant one, as he described;

'I flew towards Weert in thin layers of cloud, then returned towards Nijmegen, still between cloud layers. On emerging near Nijmegen, I saw a single aircraft about one mile in front and about 1000 ft above me. I immediately gave chase, instructing my No 2 to slow down and drop his fuel tank, being unable to do so myself due to my high speed. The enemy aircraft turned slightly to starboard and continued towards the northeast, weaving slightly from time to time. I kept out of the enemy pilot's view by keeping under his tailplane, and slowly overhauled him at an IAS of 340 mph at 8000-9000 ft.

'Whilst astern of the enemy aircraft I was only able to say it was jet-propelled, and not an Me 262. I closed to 100 yards or less, firing with my 0.5-in machine guns and cannon whilst still overtaking. I saw strikes on the port wing, port jet engine and fuselage. The enemy aircraft immediately emitted dense clouds of brownish smoke – possibly jet exhaust.

Another Spitfire XIV regularly flown by an ace was RN119/AE-J of No 402 Sqn, which is seen here at Heesch during March 1945. Canadian ace, and unit CO, Sqn Ldr Leslie Moore flew it during the early months of 1945 until he was shot down by flak and killed in MV258 whilst strafing a train on 25 March (*via J D R Rawlings*)

I continued firing and saw flashes in the smoke, breaking away at extremely close range, and being hit in the port radiator by debris.

'I next saw the enemy aircraft going down in a wide spiral to starboard, with white smoke or vapour pouring from holes all along the port wing and dark smoke from the fuselage. I could then see the long nose of the aircraft and the straight tapered wings with rounded tips, and identified it as an Arado 234. A large piece of the enemy aircraft suddenly flew off, and one person bailed out, parachute opening. The enemy aircraft steepened its dive and crashed somewhere near Enschede, being completely destroyed by the explosion. Fire from the ground was seen at this time.'

Reid's victim crashed in flames close to the HQ of AVM Harry Broadhurst, who was delighted to witness the first certain destruction of an Ar 234.

It was the start of a successful day for the Griffon Spitfire squadrons, which continued when Wg Cdr George Keefer led a sweep of Nos 130 and 350 Sqns towards Rheine. At 0745 hrs he spotted a glint below him, and leaving No 350 Sqn as top cover, he led No 130 Sqn down to intercept what turned out to be a mixed formation of 15 Bf 109 and Fw 190s. He described his first victory in the Spitfire XIV as follows;

'I picked one out and the enemy aircraft dived away. I cleared and got in behind him, giving the fighter a burst with all my guns – I saw strikes on his hood. The enemy aircraft then flicked over onto its back, went down through the cloud and I saw a parachute come out. I fired at the enemy aircraft from dead astern, and I gave him a fairly long burst.'

Following Keefer down into the attack was Flt Sgt Phil Clay, who was No 4 in the wing leader's section. He spotted an Fw 190 rolling away;

'I was able to go down inside him, and when I caught him up, the Hun did a spiral turn. I fired, but saw no strikes, and then the aircraft pulled up. I came in in line astern and from 300 yards opened fire. I saw strikes, and either the cowling or the top came off. I followed it to 5000 ft and the aircraft continued to spin down until it hit the ground and blew up.'

This was the first of Clay's six claims. Gaining his first Mk XIV victory during the same engagement was squadronmate Flt Lt Sammy Samouelle (a seven-victory ace from the campaign in North Africa), who recalled;

'I saw a long-nose Fw 190 on the tail of one of our aircraft. Both aircraft were turning steeply, but our aircraft was turning inside quite comfortably. Suddenly, our aircraft straightened up, and at the same time the Fw 190 hit our aircraft badly. I opened fire on the Fw 190 with a long burst, and saw strikes on the fuselage and wing root. The Fw 190 and our aircraft went down in a vertical dive. Our aircraft was streaming glycol and the Fw 190 was streaming black and white smoke. They both disappeared into cloud and I lost sight of them. I had to break away because there was another Fw 190 firing at me, and almost directly afterwards I saw another Fw 190 on its own. I attacked it as it turned and I got a few strikes on its port wing.'

Samouelle was credited with a destroyed and a damaged, and No 130 Sqn was credited with two more Fw 190s destroyed for the loss of two Spitfire XIVs, whose pilots were both captured. Then No 350 Sqn joined the fight and claimed a further three destroyed. The German fighters (from JG 26) had been attempting to cover Me 262 operations from Rheine, several of which were duly engaged by patrolling Tempests.

Running up at its Belgian base in early 1945 is RM683/AE-N of No 402 Sqn, which was used by Flg Off Sherk to destroy an Fw 190 near Aachen on Christmas Day 1944. The fighter remained with the squadron into the spring of 1945, when it was occasionally flown by the unit's ace CO, Sqn Ldr Don Laubman (*author's collection*)

The squadrons maintained offensive operations as the advance towards the Rhine, and preparations for the crossing of this last great obstacle, continued. Despite bitter fighting on the ground, the Spitfire XIVs saw no further air combat until the afternoon of the 13th, when No 130 Sqn escorted No 2 Group Mitchells. Flt Lt Harry Walmsley, flying 'AP-P', was leading a section near Hamm when they engaged nine Fw 190s, one of which, after a lengthy chase, he hit and saw the pilot bail out of. Another fell to Rhodesian Flt Sgt Clay, who thus registered his second victory, although his Spitfire was also damaged, while the No 4 man in the section, Flt Lt Ian Ponsford in 'AP-V', shot down an Fw 190 to open his account. He also damaged a second, later describing his first step to acedom;

'The whole section chased the aircraft for about three minutes. I selected one, and when at 400 yards dead astern, I opened fire but saw no strikes. The aircraft started to weave, and I closed to 250 yards, firing another two-three second burst at ten degrees defection, after which the enemy aircraft started to smoke. I noticed tracer passing over my port wing so I broke and, as I did so, the aircraft started to burn. Almost immediately afterwards I saw an explosion and fire on the ground.'

No 350 Sqn was also in the area, and a little earlier, its new CO, Sqn Ldr Frank Woolley, flying NH686/MN-V, shot down a long-nosed Fw 190D-9 probably from JG 26 to claim his first victory. At the time that No 130 Sqn was engaged near Hamm, Spitfire XIVs from No 402 Sqn were sweeping the Munster area, where a jet was sighted. Flg Off Howard Nicholson gave chase and opened fire 'into his starboard wing and the base of the fuselage. Smoke poured out and pieces flew off the starboard wing. I kept firing, observing many hits, and the aircraft tended to fall out of control, regaining slowly. At 2000 ft he went into a sharp dive to port'. Fortunately, his CO, Sqn Ldr Leslie Moore, saw it crash and the young Nicholson was credited with an Arado Ar 234 destroyed.

CROSSING THE RHINE

The 2nd TAF fighter squadrons gave the enemy no respite, and the airfields in northwestern Germany became no haven for the Luftwaffe. Shortly before 0900 hrs on the 19 March, No 125 Wing's leader, Wg Cdr George Keefer, led No 130 Sqn back over Rheine, where they spotted 12 Bf 109s of I./JG 27 in the circuit. Two were downed in flames, one crash-landed in a wooded area and the remaining nine were damaged. Keefer claimed one of the victories, as did Yorkshireman Flg Off Geoff Lord, who described the first of his 5.5 kills in his Combat Report;

'I went in behind one Me 109 and closed very fast. The aircraft took no evasive action and I opened fire with all guns from dead astern from about 200 yards, closing to 50 yards. I saw strikes behind the cockpit. I overshot this aircraft and I saw him crash-land on the aerodrome. I claim this aircraft damaged. After this, I pulled round and saw another '109, but as

The primitive conditions endured by the 2nd TAF units are clearly evident in this view of No 41 Sqn's dispersal at Eindhoven in early 1945 (*D S V Rake*)

I closed in I overshot him. The aircraft was trying to turn, so I pulled round on to him a second time and got behind him. The pilot was trying to do a tight turn. I turned inside him and fired from 200 yards. I saw strikes behind the cockpit and the machine blew up in the air. The pilot was able to bail out, and I saw the parachute go down and finish up in a tree about a quarter-mile to the east of the aerodrome.'

Flt Sgt Clay also damaged one of the Bf 109s.

No 125 Wing continued to remain active, as its record book noted;

'Today, the first official day of spring, was anything but a pleasant one for the Hun, for he was handed a shower of steel by the RAF. No 125 Wing was not heavily engaged, but it fulfilled its commitments. No 130 Sqn were first away at 0830 hrs to escort Mediums bombing Coesfeld, and pilots were able to report concentrated bombing. Soon after 0900 hrs No 41 Sqn sent off eight aircraft to escort a further bunch of Mediums attacking the same target, and our pilots were able to report that the bomber boys were again "bang-on". Later still, a composite team from Nos 41 and 130 Sqns went with a third box again to Coesfeld, and bombing was again reported to be good. The Hun flew no aircraft in opposition to these raids, but at times the flak was intense.'

No 41 Sqn had recently moved to Eindhoven to join Nos 130 and 350 Sqns, while No 126 Wing's No 402 Sqn was at B88 Heesch.

The Allied crossing of the Rhine – the last great natural barrier to the Reich in the west – was spearheaded by the airborne landings around Wesel. These were supported by the 21st Army Group, which began its push into Germany on 24 March under the cover of a massive air umbrella. A significant bridgehead was quickly established on the eastern banks of the Rhine. The Allied plan called for the industrial heartland of the Ruhr to be bypassed, with the focus instead being on a rapid thrust towards the Elbe and a link up with Soviet forces.

Having withdrawn to airfields further east, the Luftwaffe still found itself under constant attack from Allied fighters. And with fuel in short supply and many of their experienced leaders gone, the once mighty fighter *Geschwader* found themselves in dire straits. It was a situation that was readily exploited by the Allies, and many Spitfire XIV aces achieved this coveted status during these final, chaotic, weeks of the war.

NEMESIS OF THE LUFTWAFFE

Having helped ground forces establish a bridgehead on the eastern bank of the Rhine in the face of sometimes heavy opposition, the 2nd TAF squadrons were then freed to spread out far ahead of the 21st Army Group, hammering at enemy positions and forces as they withdrew east. Flak remained deadly, as was brought home to No 402 Sqn on 25 March when it suffered a great loss, as its operational diary recounted;

'Today, four armed recces in the Hamm/Munster area added to the squadron's score of rail and road transport destroyed. In the first show, the OC was seen to dive straight in while attacking a train, having been hit by flak. Sqn Ldr Moore will be greatly missed by both pilots and groundcrew alike.'

He had been attacking a train in the Hamm area, and was flying his regular aircraft, RM933. A few hours later, No 41 Sqn's Flt Lt Dan Reid, who had recently destroyed an Arado jet, was hit by flak and wounded – he was later awarded a DFC.

However, in spite of the dangers from ground fire, the Spitfire XIV squadrons took a steady toll of the enemy. Indeed, whenever the units engaged the Luftwaffe, the combination of the aircraft's superb performance and the high experience levels of their pilots often made the fights very one-sided. This was well illustrated during several clashes on the afternoon of 28 March, one of which involved No 130 Sqn. Eight Spitfires from the unit had been tasked with flying an armed reconnaissance mission over Gutersloh, and at 1645 hrs, near Warendorf, they met 15 Fw 190D-9s. Led by Flt Lt Harry Walmsley, the Spitfire pilots waded in, reportedly 'with great enthusiasm', and claimed seven destroyed, with three others damaged. However, in the confusion of battle, the losses to IV./JG 26 had been overestimated somewhat.

Among the successful pilots, and making his first steps towards acedom, was 22-year-old New Zealander Flt Sgt Brian Woodman, while the Fw 190 that Walmsley destroyed gave him ace status. Flt Sgt Phillip Clay downed his third victim, as did Wt Off Joseph Boulton, who would also eventually tally five claims. Of his first successful combat, Flt Sgt Woodman said;

'Just after 1645 hrs we were flying north when aircraft which I identified as long-nosed Fw 190s passed

Flt Lt Harry Walmsley became an ace on 28 March 1945 when, in an action fought to the south of Warendorf during an armed reconnaissance, he shot down an Fw 190D-9 (*via M Goodman*)

us on the port side, travelling in the opposite direction. We broke round into them, and I found there were three of them in front of me. I picked on the last one of the three and climbed after him. I opened fire at about 800 yards and I saw strikes on the wing.

'I then got onto the second one from about 30 degrees angle off and opened fire again from about 800 yards. I closed in to about 400 yards and fired again from dead astern whilst climbing. I saw strikes on the wing roots on the port side. There was a burst of yellow flame from where I had seen the strikes. The aircraft went over onto its back and it went down out of control, and I saw a trail of smoke right down until the aircraft hit the ground. It finished up in a field, where it continued to burn, and there was just a mass of red embers.'

Wt Off Boulton saw it falling to pieces under the weight of Woodman's fire and, burning furiously, pass within 50 yards of his own Spitfire.

However, the day's most significant event was a change in Allied strategic priorities that no longer made Berlin, against which Field Marshal Montgomery's 21st Army Group was driving, the objective. Thus, instead of spearheading the assault from the west, the 21st Army Group was now to conduct what amounted to a huge flanking operation, while US forces occupied the Ruhr and Berlin was left entirely to the Soviet offensive.

In reality, for 2nd TAF units little changed, and Spitfire XIV units, including Nos 2 and 430 Sqns, remained operating at full tilt. Flt Lt Cowan of No 402 Sqn was successful on the 30th when he downed an Fw 190 near Oldenburg, while during an armed reconnaissance in the same area the following morning Flg Off Robert Lawson downed the Fw 190D-9s of Oberleutnante Burkhardt and Raith from 5./JG 26, and Flt Lt Bruce Innes claimed another.

THE ACTION MOUNTS

April 1945 was to prove one of the busiest and most successful months for the Spitfire XIV units, and the action began early. On the 2nd, No 350

No 130 Sqn's Flt Lt Walmsley was flying this particular Spitfire XIV when he 'made ace' on 28 March 1945. He had also used it to claim his fourth victory 15 days earlier (*via C H Thomas*)

Also successful during No 130 Sqn's combat on 28 March was Flt Sgt Brian Woodman, who claimed the first of his four and one shared victories when he destroyed an Fw 190 on this date (*via B Cull*)

Sqn returned to Eindhoven from its Armament Practice Camp in the UK, and a few days later it moved with the rest of No 125 Wing to B106 Twente, on the Dutch-German border, just 24 hours after the base had been captured! Ten days later it moved onto German soil when it occupied B118 Celle, where the unit remained until war's end.

In No 126 Wing, No 402 Sqn also moved into Germany when it took up residence at B108 Rheine – one of its former targets – on the 12th, before moving on to B116 Wunstorf three days later. It remained here until VE-Day.

British and Canadian forces had advanced as far as a line from Lingen to Osnabruck by early April, and having hastily re-established themselves further east, Luftwaffe fighter units began reappearing over the front once more, albeit in relatively small numbers.

The newly-returned No 350 Sqn returned to action too, losing an aircraft to flak on the 4th, but during an armed reconnaissance the following day in the Aschendorf-Lingen area, the Belgian unit engaged some Fw 190s. Flg Off Muls and Flt Sgt Neulinger shared in the destruction of a Focke-Wulf, although the unit lost Flg Off Cresswell-Turner in return when his aircraft was hit by flak and he became a PoW. No 41 Sqn's Flt Lt Bill Stowe, who would become an ace before April was out, also had a narrow escape when his aircraft was hit in the spinner and propeller by the ever-deadly light flak.

No 402 Sqn was also in action shortly after No 350 Sqn, claiming two fighters destroyed and a number damaged in a combat near Lingen. Flg Off Ratcliffe later recalled the demise of his victim;

'I saw tracers going into cockpit and watched him go down. The aeroplane hit the deck and burst into flames. It was an Me 109, and I did not see the pilot get out.'

No 41 Sqn pilot Flt Lt Derek Rake recalled his impressions of operations during the final weeks of the war in Europe;

'By this stage, our armoured columns were breaking out across the North German plain, and our brief on almost every sortie was to attack anything that moved ahead of the "bomb line". The tanks were going forward so fast that we were often given a revised "bomb line" by our GCI controller "Kenway" after we were airborne. Sometimes, the tanks even got ahead of this, and we had to pull out of attacks when we saw the colours of the day displayed on the tops of tanks and armoured vehicles.'

On the 6th, Flt Lt Tony Gaze joined No 41 Sqn as 'A' Flight commander. The unit was by now flying the Mk XIVE, which had had the 0.303-in machine guns of the standard Griffon Spitfire replaced with more effective 0.50-in weapons. The aircraft was also equipped with an improved gyro gunsight that greatly assisted in air-to-air gunnery, although by now No 41 Sqn spent most of its time attacking ground targets. Unit CO, Sqn Ldr Douglas Benham, having taken his score to eight, was replaced by newly-promoted Sqn Ldr John Shepherd at this time too. No 402 Sqn also received an experienced new commander in the shape of 16-victory ace Sqn Ldr Don Laubman on 7 April, and he flew his first mission in RM804 48 hours later.

No 130 Sqn was also active, and on the evening of the 10th it sent out aircraft from Twente to patrol over Nordholz and Wenzendorf. A few minutes after 1930 hrs, and shortly before dark, squadron CO, and Kiwi,

NH745/EB-V, latterly flown by No 41 Sqn's CO, Sqn Ldr Douglas Benham, was one of the first Mk XIVs to be fitted with a bubble hood. Note the squadron's badge applied to the nose in red (*D I Benham via C H Thomas*)

One of the most successful pilots flying with No 41 Sqn in the spring of 1945 was Australian ace Flt Lt Tony Gaze, who, on 12 April, shared in the destruction of an Ar 234 jet bomber with Flt Lt Derek Rake to add to the Me 262 he had destroyed in February whilst flying with No 610 Sqn (*F A O Gaze*)

Sqn Ldr Martin Hume shot down a Ju 188 as it was landing at Stade – the bomber was his fifth claim, three of which had been confirmed as destroyed. He gave the following description of this, his final claim;

'I immediately went down on it and the top gunner opened fire from extreme range, but his fire was to port, and I continued firing till I closed the range to 300 yards. I saw strikes on the port engine and on the port wing root, and both the engine and the wing caught fire. I broke away, knowing that it was impossible for the aircraft to carry on. It managed to fly on for a mile and then it turned to port. Its turn steepened and then it crashed into a field two miles east of Stade. There were no survivors.'

Hume handed over to another successful pilot, Sqn Ldr Frank Woolley, when he returned to base.

12 April saw Flt Lt Tony Gaze again encounter a German jet, although this time it outpaced him and he then had to avoid the attentions of its covering Fw 190 patrol. Two days later, however, when in company with Flt Lt Derek Rake, it was a different story, as the latter described to the author especially for this volume;

'My log book confirms that I shared in the destruction of an Ar 234 with Flt Lt Tony Gaze. We took off from Twente and climbed through quite a lot of cloud towards Delmenhorst-Verden. Tony was leading the flight. We came out on top at around 20,000 ft, and as we levelled out, I recall seeing what I recognised as an Arado 234 twin jet break cloud to port ahead of us and below. I was in the near perfect position for a quarter attack.

'My Spitfire, a Mk XIVE, was fitted with a gyro gunsight with a ranging twist grip on the throttle. As I dived towards the target I was able to position the jet within the diamond markers on the gunsight – thus having the correct range and

53

deflection to open fire. My opening burst hit the starboard engine, and it was smoking as it rolled over and dived towards the cloud. I got in one or two more bursts as I followed it down. I believe that I claimed the "kill", but think that Tony must have had a share in finishing it off.'

Derek Rake was flying MV267, while Tony Gaze was in SM823/EB-E. He too recalled the combat;

'I shouldn't have got the Arado really because the chap didn't know what he was doing, and tried to outclimb us. If he'd stuck his nose down, he'd have gone. The reason I shared it was that the Arado proved to be almost impossible to shoot at with the gyro gunsight. If you got absolutely plumb astern of the jet on a chase, you got into the slipstream or vortices off the wingtips, and you could only get off a half-second burst before the Spitfire started to be twisted about. With an ordinary sight, you wouldn't have been that accurate, exactly behind. I kept doing little tiny squirts, which knocked one engine out, and the other was smoking so I don't think he'd have got very far.'

On 14 April No 41 Sqn's CO, Sqn Ldr John Shepherd, also encountered one of the number of advanced fighters the Luftwaffe had developed – albeit in very favourable circumstances! John Shepherd, who was flying SM826/EB-B near Nordholz airfield, spotted a Bf 110 towing an Me 163 Komet rocket fighter that was being piloted by Oberfeldwebel Werner Nelte. The latter had previously served on the Eastern Front with 1./JG 54, where he had scored seven victories, and had later joined I./JG 400 to fly the Komet. Shepherd promptly shot down the tug and then turned on the tiny Me 163, as he recalled in his combat report;

'I was leading "Kudos Red" section (three aircraft), one having turned back with engine trouble. On the second leg of the sweep, when passing over Nordholz airfield, two aircraft were seen to take off. Diving on them, I recognised them as an Me 163 being towed by an Me 110. I was closing very rapidly, but managed to get a short burst in on the Me 110, seeing strikes on the port engine and cockpit. The Me 110 went into a left hand diving turn, turned over onto its back and crashed into a field, bursting into flames. The Me 163 appeared to break away from the Me 110 and make a wide left hand turn, finally diving straight in about three fields away from the Me 110.'

Spitfire XIVs MV260/EB-P (nearest) and SM826/EB-B of No 41 Sqn are prepared for their next sorties during April. SM826 was an 'ace' in its own right, having been used by Sqn Ldr John Shepherd to destroy a Bf 110 and an Me 163 on 14 April, whilst Tony Gaze and Pat Coleman made a total of three claims while flying it later that same month (*via C F Shores*)

In spite of his lack of power, and low altitude, Nelte managed to pull the Komet out of its dive at the last moment and crash-land, although the Bf 110 crew were killed.

Elsewhere that same day, No 402 Sqn lost another CO just eight days after taking control of the unit when Sqn Ldr Don Laubman was forced to bail out over enemy territory after attacking enemy half-tracks. Having set one of the latter on fire, his aircraft was hit by debris as the armoured vehicle exploded and he had to take to his parachute. 2nd TAF's top-scoring pilot since D-Day (all of his 14 and 2 shared kills having come flying Spitfire IXs with No 412 Sqn), Laubman spent the remaining weeks of the war as a PoW. He was replaced on 16 April by fellow ace Sqn Ldr Don Gordon, who had claimed a shared kill earlier that same day on his last patrol with No 411 Sqn.

ROCKETS AND SUBMARINES

After the last of the Mk XIV squadrons had departed for the Continent in late 1944, Fighter Command had been devoid of Griffon-engined Spitfire units. However, throughout that year the Spitfire had undergone a major redesign, resulting in production of the Mk XXI. Gone was the classical elliptical wing, its place having been taken by a strengthened new wing that at last boasted additional fuel tanks to extend range. The aircraft also featured a redesigned tail and a beefed up undercarriage, as well as four 20 mm Hispano cannon as standard. Finally, the Mk XXI had an impressive top speed of 450+ mph at 26,000 ft.

One of the original Griffon Spitfire units, No 91 Sqn was selected as the first to introduce this potent new Mark into frontline service. Now based at Manston, it had reverted to Spitfire IXs the previous summer. The first two Mk XXIs (LA210 and LA212) were delivered on 4 January 1945, although No 91 Sqn was forced to continue flying 'Ramrod' sorties with its Mk IXs, as the Mk XXI was initially prohibited from being flown over enemy territory by Fighter Command HQ.

On 1 March Sqn Ldr Mick Maskill assumed command of No 91 Sqn, and on 8 April he led the unit to Ludham, in north Norfolk – only its new Spitfire XXIs accompanied the squadron north from Manston. The first

The only 'victory' claimed by a Spitfire XXI was made by LA223/DL-Y of No 91 Sqn when 4.5-victory ace Flt Lt John Draper used it to claim a share in the destruction of an enemy midget submarine off the Dutch coast on 26 April 1945 (*P R Arnold collection*)

sorties began two days later, when a pair flew an armed reconnaissance over Holland and spotted several minesweepers and barges off the coast. Four more Spitfire XXIs were scrambled to attack the vessels, but Flt Lt Roy Cruickshank and Flg Off Johnny Faulkner were both shot down by flak as they attacked the ships off Den Helder. The pilots bailed out into the sea and were quickly rescued and returned to the unit.

Despite No 91 Sqn's first day of operations with the powerful new aircraft not being a total success, the unit diary noted, 'The pilots like their Spitfire XXIs!' The following day the unit's diary recorded that one of the aces remaining with the squadron, Flt Lt John Draper, had married a WAAF!

With little air activity, the squadron was tasked with searching for V2 rocket launch sites, code named Operation 'Big Ben', over Holland. It was also ordered to fly a series of anti-submarine patrols – certainly a role that the Spitfire was never designed to perform! German one and two-man midget submarines had been harassing Allied vessels in the Scheldt Estuary and off the Dutch coast, so searching for submarines and V2s became No 91 Sqn's main tasks in the final weeks of the war in Europe. Two-dozen such sorties were flown on 13 April alone.

Two days later further 'Big Ben' and anti-submarine sorties were flown, and Sqn Ldr Maskill was awarded the DFC. During the afternoon of 17 April a pair of Spitfire XXIs, led by Flt Lt Cruickshank in LA223/ DL-Y, were scrambled after an unidentified 'plot' which subsequently turned out to be a friendly air-sea rescue Warwick.

Operations over Holland continued daily, and at 0945 hrs on the 26th, a pair of Spitfire XXIs flown by V1 ace Flt Lt Bill Marshall (in LA252) and 4.5-victory ace Flt Lt John Draper (in LA223/DL-Y) set out for the Dutch coast on yet another anti-submarine patrol. Having flown down to the Scheldt, they then headed north, and off the Hook of Holland John

Another of No 91 Sqn's Spitfire XXIs is seen parked in the Ludham dispersal in late April 1945. LA200/DL-E was written off on 12 May when its pilot, Flg Off Geoffrey Kay, was killed whilst aerobating in the fighter near the airfield (*via E B Morgan*)

Draper spotted a *Biber* submarine departing the mole. The pair turned around and set up for an attack, as the combat report of the Spitfire XXI's only tangible success against the enemy described for posterity;

'The Midget sub was then some 250-300 yards off shore, and despite moderate, but accurate, light flak from gun positions on the mole, the section attacked with cannon. Diving from 1000 ft down to 50 ft, both pilots obtained strikes on the superstructure and around the conning tower, which brought the sub almost to a standstill. The section made a second attack, this time in a northerly direction, from the same height. Strikes were again scored, and as a result of this second attack the sub was seen to sink, leaving wreckage and a large patch of oil on the surface.'

Upon returning to base, however, the pilots' low-level beat up was met with the disapproval of the visiting sector commander! Five days later No 91 Sqn flew its final operation.

RACE TO THE ELBE

As the Allies advanced so some PoWs were liberated, among them No 350 Sqn's old CO, Sqn Ldr Terry Spencer, who had quickly resumed command of the unit – Sqn Ldr Frank Woolley in turn transferred to No 130 Sqn as its CO. Spencer's second tenure was also brief. On 19 April, he led his squadron on a strafing attack on an airfield near Buchen. Having destroyed a Ju 88, he then swept out over the Bay of Wismar, where he spotted a ship and 'attacked the tanker with cannon and machine guns. Two German warships were in the lee of the hills and in the shade, and I never saw them. They opened up with everything possible. My Spitfire was blown in two over the water. My 'chute was blown out of its pack and I landed in the bay in time to see the front part of my Spitfire crash on land!'

Injured, and once more a PoW, Spencer was eventually liberated in early May. However, for his offensive spirit and conspicuous gallantry, he was awarded an immediate DFC.

No 130 Sqn's pilots take time out for a photo after moving to Celle in April 1945. Standing at far right is Flt Lt Bill Stowe, and third to his right is fellow ace Plt Off Freddie Edwards, whilst under the propeller holding a camera is the CO, Sqn Ldr Frank Woolley (*W N Stowe via C H Thomas*)

The fighter reconnaissance units equipped with the Spitfire XIV were also flying flat out, ranging well ahead of the advancing troops and bringing back much useful tactical intelligence information. A new unit carrying out these missions in April was No 268 Sqn at Twente, which had swapped its Mustangs for Griffon Spitfires early that month.

Although flak posed the main threat to pilots flying these sorties, they also occasionally encountered enemy fighters too. Indeed, No 430 Sqn's Flt Lt Warren Middleton clashed with an Fw 190 near Uelzen on the 15 April during a reconnaissance flight, as he later recalled;

'I broke to port and closed on his tail. I opened fire at a range of 450 yards dead astern, and closed to 250 yards. I saw strikes on the fuselage, the cowl top flew off, the aircraft trailed black smoke and then burst into flame and I saw it crash and blow up on the ground.'

The following day, the No 125 Wing squadrons were out again, losing two aircraft in the morning. In the late evening, Wg Cdr Keefer led a section from No 41 Sqn (which had just arrived at Celle) on a sweep up towards Schwerin, and flying at 7000 ft near Hagenow, he spotted three Fw 190s dived on them. 'I dived to attack and fired at one aircraft, observing strikes. The German pilot flew through his own flak over Hagenow'. Keefer broke off his attack due to the flak, which meant that he could only claim the enemy fighter as damaged. Meanwhile, Flt Lt John Wilkinson (in MV249) had followed the other two Fw 190s down;

During the many sweeps conducted in late April, No 125 Wing leader Wg Cdr George Keefer flew his personal Spitfire MV263/GCK. He shot down two enemy fighters and destroyed no fewer than five on the ground with this machine in April 1945. Flt Lt Peter Cowell is seen here in front of it (*P Cowell via C H Thomas*)

With a total of eight victories to his name, Sqn Ldr John Shepherd (standing near the wing trailing edge, alongside the cockpit) was the fourth most successful pilot on the Griffon Spitfire (*via C H Thomas*)

'The Fw 190s broke to port into our attack and we followed round, diving and turning inside them. I picked the starboard aircraft and fired a two-second burst at him from about 250 yards, in his turn. I saw strikes on the port side of the engine and cockpit. Having too much speed, I overshot under his tail, but tightened my turn and pulled in behind him again. He straightened out and I gave him a seven-second burst, getting strikes on the engine and cockpit. The aircraft turned to starboard streaming oil, which covered my windscreen. I fired one two-second blind burst at him and he went from a gentle dive into a field between two woods and burst into 200 yards of flame.'

In spite of the war having just three weeks to run, this was Flt Lt Wilkinson's first step to achieving ace status. Sqn Ldr John Shepherd then chased the third Fw 190, and getting into position at low-level, he too shot it down for his eighth success. No 41 Sqn was in action again early the following morning when, shortly after 0630 hrs, Flt Lt Tony Gaze and Flg Off F M Hegarty found a Ju 88 near Lubeck. After Gaze had run out of ammunition following a series of passes, Hegarty, in SM826/EB-P, shot the bomber down to claim his third and final victory.

During a later sortie, Plt Off Pat Coleman destroyed another Ju 188 during a strafing attack, while over Vechlin at around 1400 hrs, No 130 Sqn's Flt Lt Harry Walmsley strafed Ju 252 GC+BK that belonged to the enemy's test establishment. His unit's sweep over the area was followed a few minutes later by five more Spitfires XIVs from No 350 Sqn that bounced Fw 190Ds from II./JG 26 to the south of Hamburg – Flt Sgt Andre Kicq shot one down for his first victory.

No 125 Wing pilots had another successful day on the 18th when, in mid-afternoon, No 130 Sqn destroyed four Fi 156 Storch observation aircraft on the ground at Wustrow, with Walmsley claiming two. A few hours later Wg Cdr Keefer led the squadron back to Parchim, where they spotted a group of 11 Bf 109s preparing to take off. In the subsequent strafing attacks Keefer personally claimed five of them destroyed, although he was outscored by Flg Off Trevorrow;

'I fired into the middle of the bunch. I saw strikes immediately and there was a big flame and then an explosion. Debris flew up about 200 ft, and as I flew through it my aircraft was hit. I set course for base, and on looking back I saw another explosion and there was a pillar of black smoke rising then to about 500-600 ft.'

He claimed the remaining six destroyed, although his Spitfire had been hit by debris. The action had been witnessed by No 125 Wing CO, and one of the RAF's leading aces, Gp Capt Johnnie Johnson;

'I saw Wg Cdr Keefer and Flg Off Trevorrow make their attack on the eleven '109s. Four were hit and commenced to burn. I then orbited the aerodrome at 6000 ft and saw several large explosions as the remainder of

One of the most successful Belgian pilots during the spring of 1945 was Flt Sgt Andre Kicq of No 350 Sqn, who claimed two and one shared victories – the latter being an Ar 234 jet (*A van Haute*)

the tightly packed formations caught fire. All eleven aircraft were completely burned out and as we passed the aerodrome twenty minutes later a dense pall of smoke reached 10,000 ft.'

That same day, No 350 Sqn inflicted more pain on the enemy in their own backyard when they attacked an airfield near Hamburg. Led by Flt Lt Pat Bangerter, Plt Off Des Watkins and Flt Sgt Gigot destroyed four Ju 88s and damaged an Fw 190. For the once mighty Luftwaffe, there was now nowhere to hide from the deadly attentions of Allied air power.

18 April also saw No 402 Sqn's new CO, Sqn Ldr Don Gordon, fly his first operation – an armed reconnaissance in RM814. The following day he completed two more sweeps,

During April 1945, No 402 Sqn had three COs in little over a week! The final one was Canadian ace Sqn Ldr Don 'Chunky' Gordon (seen here examining an abandoned German panzer), who claimed his final victory with the unit when he shot down an unfortunate Fieseler Fi 156 Storch on 3 May (*Canadian Forces*)

and in the evening a third mission was flown at the controls of RM858. During the course of the latter mission No 402 Sqn's Flg Off McConnell intercepted a Ju 88, which he promptly shot down, while Flt Lt Dutton claimed an Fw 190 and others were damaged in a dogfight.

In No 126 Wing No 401 Sqn, led by ace Sqn Ldr Bill Klersy, had also begun to slowly re-equip with Mk XIVs, but the unit was still in the process of fully converting when the war came to end.

On 19 April, whilst flying yet another armed reconnaissance mission, Flt Lt Tony Gaze and his section had an unusual encounter. They chased an Me 262 that they reported was apparently leading what they initially identified as a V1 flying bomb in formation. However, afterwards it was assessed that the aircraft was probably a new He 162, a handful of which were based at Leck. This was one of the very few encounters that the RAF had with the *Volksjager*, an example of which was apparently shot down by a Tempest of No 222 Sqn shortly after Gaze's sighting.

Then, in the early evening of the 19th, it was No 130 Sqn's turn to mix it with the enemy when, during a sweep towards Wismar, Flt Lt Ian Ponsford, in 'AP-V', bagged an Fw 190 to claim his second victory. The newly promoted Wt Off Phillip Clay, in RM766, downed another for his fourth confirmed kill, but both he and Flg Off Murphy were then in turn shot down by German fighters and became PoWs – Clay was decorated with a DFC soon afterwards.

The next day, when flying 'AP-D', Ian Ponsford was even more successful. During a sweep towards Hamburg, his section was attacked by some long-nosed Fw 190D-9s near Oranienburg and he shot down one of them. Moments later he went to the assistance of his leader, Flt Lt Walmsley, who was hotly engaged with two more enemy fighters. Ponsford probably destroyed a second Focke-Wulf and damaged a third. Harry Walmsley, flying 'AP-F', also destroyed one of the Fw 190s, and so

No 41 Sqn's Flt Lt John Wilkinson was flying Spitfire XIV RM931/EB-U when, on 20 April, near Oranienburg, he shared in the destruction of two Fw 190s. It is believed that he is the pilot seen here posing alongside the aircraft (*via C F Shores*)

by a short head over No 41 Sqn's Sqn Ldr John Shepherd became the first pilot to claim five kills with the Spitfire XIV. Then, minutes later, Plt Off Pat Coleman claimed his second victory by destroying another Fw 190.

That evening more successes came the way of the Mk XIV squadrons when Wg Cdr Keefer led his No 125 Wing on a sweep. Having spread out, some 30 minutes after take-off, when at 7000 ft over the Kremmen Forest north of Oranienburg, Sqn Ldr John Shepherd of No 41 Sqn spotted an enemy formation below him. He led his men down;

'In the ensuing dogfight, five Fws were shot down by the squadron. I fired at one from approximately 200 yards, getting strikes on its cockpit and engine. This aircraft went down in flames.'

Shepherd reformed the squadron and led them north, before returning to the Oranienburg area, where they spotted more fighters and further chases resulted. One of the aircraft forced down was an Me 262 that was attacked by Wt Off Rossow, although he was only credited with a 'probable'. Sqn Ldr John Shepherd continued;

'At this time an Fw 190 was sighted by my No 2, which we chased. Closing on him, I opened fire from about 200 yards, range decreasing. I got strikes on his cockpit and engine, causing him to catch fire and his undercarriage to drop. I broke away when this happened, and Flt Lt Wilkinson – my No 2 – carried on the attack and followed him down. This aircraft went down in flames and crashed in the woods northwest of Oranienburg aerodrome.'

This shared victory was Shepherd's fifth with the Spitfire XIV and John Wilkinson's third success. Meanwhile, Wg Cdr Keefer was with No 130 Sqn's element, and at 5000 ft near Wittstock he got his penultimate kill;

'I was flying with No 130 Sqn and was leading Red Section. We spotted two Me 109s slightly above us at "12 o'clock" to us, going the same way. I picked one and opened fire from dead astern. I saw strikes on the fuselage. I gave him another burst at closer range, whereupon the aircraft caught fire, crashed into a field and exploded.'

Also claiming his penultimate victory was No 130 Sqn's Flt Lt 'Sammy' Samouelle, who destroyed a Bf 109G;

'I caught one of the aircraft at 8000 ft, closed in and opened fire at 300 yards from astern. I saw strikes all round the cockpit and on the back of the aircraft. There was a big red flash, white smoke came out and I found myself flying through debris. I had to pull up sharply to avoid hitting the

Joining No 125 Wing as leader during April 1945 was the legendary Wg Cdr Johnnie Johnson, who, with 34 and seven shared victories, was one of the most successful Allied fighter pilots of the war (*Canadian Forces*)

On moving to No 125 Wing, Johnson adopted MV268 as his personal aircraft, which was soon carrying his initials on its fuselage as befitting his position (*H Halliday via L Milberry*)

aircraft. When I was able to look again, it was in a flat spin, and at 4000 ft the pilot bailed out.'

No 350 Sqn also engaged the enemy on 20 April during a sweep of the German capital. Northwest of Berlin, the Belgians spotted 15 Fw 190s, probably from IV.(*Sturm*)/JG 3, and in the ensuing fight the superb Spitfire XIVs once again held the honours – amongst the enemy pilots lost was Defence of the Reich *experte* Feldwebel Willi Maximowitz. No 350 Sqn claimed four Fw 190s destroyed and two damaged.

Taking his first step to acedom during the course of this mission was 'Yellow' Section leader, 23-year-old Welshman Plt Off Des Watkins, flying RB155/MN-C;

'I noticed two Fw 190s coming towards me, slightly below us. I selected the one on the port side, made a sharp turn to port and gave it a quick burst as it was overshooting me. I observed strikes on the starboard mainplane. The aircraft then rolled onto its back, and in the process caught a long burst in its belly. The aircraft turned into a tight spiral and spun towards the ground – I saw it blow up.'

The Belgian squadron gained another new CO three days later when Harry Walmsley was promoted to squadron leader. However, his final day with No 130 Sqn – 23 April – was to be a memorable one. In the early evening he led six Spitfires on an armed reconnaissance towards the Neustadt area and Parchim airfield, over which he spotted a pair of small Bf 108 Taifun liaison aircraft. He quickly dived after the first one;

'I attacked from the port quarter. I did not see any strikes, but the two occupants of the machine immediately bailed out and the aircraft crashed to the north of the aerodrome.'

He then led his formation off to the west, where he spotted the second Taifun;

'I dived to attack and the aircraft went under my nose. I then spotted him again at zero feet and made another attack. Although I did not hit him, he tried to land in a field, went up on his nose at speed and broke up.'

SOVIET ENCOUNTERS

23 April had also seen No 125 Wing, led by Gp Capt Johnnie Johnson, fly a historic sweep over Berlin, where the Spitfire pilots met 40 Soviet Yak-9 fighters. Johnson recorded in his classic book *Wing Leader*;

'I led the wing on the Berlin show at the first opportunity. For this epic occasion our first team took to the air. George (Keefer – the Wing Leader) led a squadron and Tony Gaze flew with me again – the first time since we flew together in Bader's Wing. We swept to Berlin at a couple of thousand feet above the ground, over a changing sunlit countryside of desolate heathland, small lakes and large forests, with the empty, double ribbon of the autobahn lying close on our starboard side. Tony Gaze spotted '50+ at "two o'clock"' – they turned out to be Russians.'

Another Spitfire XIV squadron also began operations on this day when Sqn Ldr Jim Prendergast of Wunstorf-based No 414 Sqn flew a reconnaissance to Bremerhaven. Then, in the early afternoon, Flt Lt D I Hall led another pair on an abortive sortie. Although flying in the reconnaissance role, 'Sammy' Hall, who had achieved three victories in late 1944 flying the Spitfire IX, would also soon become an ace.

The Spitfire XIV units' increasing toll of the Luftwaffe continued on 24 April too when, a little after 0600 hrs, six aircraft from No 130 Sqn left Celle on yet another armed reconnaissance mission. Just before 0700 hrs they spotted an Fw 190 that was chased back to Neustadt, where more were seen orbiting. Three were destroyed, with 'Sammy' Samouelle claiming his final victory and Flt Sgt Brian Woodman getting his second, as he later described in his Combat Report;

'I got within range and gave the enemy aircraft a short burst. It rolled over to starboard and crashed into a field. By this time there were two or three Fw 190s round the circuit, and I saw one with wheels down at about 1000 ft. I closed in to 300 yards, and just as the aircraft got its wheels up I opened fire from dead astern. I got strikes all over the rear of the fuselage and it crashed into a village northwest of the aerodrome.'

Woodman also damaged a second Focke-Wulf. Soon afterwards six more pilots from No 130 Sqn, led by Sqn Ldr Frank Woolley, headed towards Wismar, where the CO spotted another hapless Bf 108 that was shot down. His wingman, Wt Off Coverdale, also bagged an Fw 190. That afternoon, No 41 Sqn, led by Flt Lt Peter Cowell, swept east and damaged four Ar 196 floatplanes seen at anchor on the large Ratzeburger See. No 350 Sqn also rapidly increased its score on the 24th when, during a mid-afternoon sweep led by Gp Capt Johnnie Johnson, Flg Off van Eeckhoudt and Plt Off Des Watkins destroyed an He 111 that they encountered. The latter wrote;

'I saw an He 111 immediately ahead of me flying north at 50 ft. I closed to some 50 yards behind him and gave his port engine a long burst from dead astern. A mass of debris flew off and I had to break port to avoid it.'

Having broken away, Des Watkins looked back and saw that the Heinkel had crash-landed in a field, its loss of an engine at such low altitude making it uncontrollable. He duly 'flew down and set it on fire in the field'.

That evening No 350 Sqn CO Sqn Ldr Harry Walmsley led some of his pilots, along with others from No 130 Sqn, towards the famous test centre at Rechlin. Walmsley shared an Fw 190 with Flt Lt de Patoul, who, over Blankensee airfield a few minutes later, was hit by flak and bailed out to become a PoW – such was the random hazard of such low-level sorties. No 130 Sqn destroyed a brace of Fw 190s, one of which fell to future ace Flt Lt Bill Stowe, who also shared a Bf 109. However, it was not all plain sailing, as over the Lubeck area No 41 Sqn's Spitfires encountered Soviet aircraft, which promptly attacked. Tony Gaze was in turn almost forced to fire on a Petlyakov Pe-2 twin-engined bomber!

On the morning of 25 April many more armed reconnaissance sweeps were mounted, with No 130 Sqn having yet another big day. In the Schwerin area, which was to prove a fruitful hunting area for the Spitfire XIV squadrons over the next few weeks, Wt Off Joseph Boulton attacked a Ju 87 as it took off, forcing it back down. Then over Rechlin some 15 minutes later Flt Lt Ian Ponsford attacked a Bf 109;

'I then went down with my "No 2" (Wt Off Coverdale) and I saw an Me 109G with its wheels down making a slight turn to port. I closed to about 50 yards and started firing at 20 degrees off. I saw strikes all round the cockpit, engine and wings. The aircraft began to pour white and black smoke and it rolled slowly over onto its back, crashed into some woods and exploded as it hit the ground.'

This was Ponsford's fourth victory. Also successful was Plt Off Freddie Edwards, who damaged an Fw 190 on the ground, while Flt Lt Bill Stowe and Wt Off Ockenden damaged others, including an Me 262. The latter recounted his attack on the jet;

'I fired at it from a steep angle, and just as I pressed the tit I saw a parachute streaming out behind the aircraft, with the air from the slipstream filling the parachute.'

As the M 262 was not positively seen to have been wrecked, frustratingly for Ockenden it was only credited as a probable. Equally as frustrated was No 41 Sqn's Flt Lt Peter Cowell, who was to end the war one victory short of acedom;

'I observed two Me 262s flying in an easterly direction in line abreast, and I turned in sharply after them as they passed over the top of me. They opened up and dived for the deck. I followed them doing 440 mph in the dive and 400 mph on the deck, and was closing slowly. The Me 262 on the starboard side did a turn to starboard and put his wheels and flaps down with the intention of doing a right hand circuit to land west-to-east. I was therefore able to cut him off and make a short head-on attack. No results were observed.

'I then broke sharply to port and was able to make a 60-degree beam attack as he continued in his circuit. I observed strikes in the cockpit area and between the starboard nacelle and the fuselage, and a large sheet of flame issued from this point. The pilot of the aircraft then landed his machine on the grass beside the runway, where it slewed round to starboard and volumes of white smoke issued from it. The other machine landed on the runway in the opposite direction, and it appeared that either the starboard tyre burst or the starboard leg collapsed, for the aircraft slewed round off the runway onto the grass, dragging its starboard wing tip on the ground.'

He was credited with a probable and a damaged.

Seen at Eindhoven on 5 April is No 41 Sqn Spitfire XIV RM797/EB-E, which was usually flown by Flt Lt Bill Stowe. The latter moved over to No 130 Sqn as a flight commander in mid-April, and he had claimed two and two shared victories with this unit by VE-Day (*W N Stowe via C H Thomas*)

More action for No 130 Sqn came during a lunchtime sortie, with Plt Off Freddie Edwards claiming his first kill when he downed an Fw 190 over Prizwalk, as did Wg Cdr Keefer, who claimed his final success. Also engaged near Rechlin at this time was No 350 Sqn, and its CO downed another Fw 190, but the honours went to Plt Off Emile Pauwels;

'I opened full throttle and followed "Red Leader" as he went in first to attack. I selected two aircraft on the port side, which I identified as Fw 190s, flying in line astern and started chasing them as they dived down. I closed in very quickly behind them and fired one long burst at the rear one from dead astern within 250-200 yards. I observed strikes on the cockpit and wing roots and debris flew off, with black smoke pouring out. The aircraft went onto its side and the pilot bailed out – a fraction of a second afterwards the aircraft blew up in the air.'

He then went after another Fw 190, hitting it with a long burst that caused it to flick over and explode when it struck the ground.

As these units landed, a patrol from No 41 Sqn departed. At 1400 hrs, Flg Off Pat Coleman and his wingman, Wt Off Chalmers, shot down a Ju 188, as the former described;

'Wt Off Chalmers dived in pursuit. I followed behind and saw him obtain good strikes on the aircraft, setting its starboard engine on fire. I took some good photos by pressing the independent camera button whilst still out of guns range. The aircraft was slowed down and I closed quickly, firing using the gyro gunsight. It descended, with me behind, almost to tree-top level. I scored strikes and broke away. The aircraft attempted to crash-land at Rechlin airfield, whilst Wt Off Chalmers once more attacked. It crash-landed, wheels up in the centre of the 'drome.'

Meanwhile, No 130 Sqn's CO, Sqn Ldr Woolley, found an unfortunate Siebel Si 204 twin-engined light transport, which he swiftly sent down to claim his penultimate victory. He was, frustratingly, to end the war with four confirmed victories too.

By now the advanced elements of the 21st Army Group had pushed far across the north German plain, closed on the Elbe and captured the port city of Bremen. One consequence of this endless advancing to the north and east was that the number of airfield targets was rapidly diminishing. Allied fighters were by now roaming almost at will over northern Germany, including the Spitfire XIVs of No 350 Sqn. On 26 April, during a lunchtime patrol, the unit claimed two Fw 190s, with the share credited to Sqn Ldr Walmsley being his final success of the war.

At around the same time Sqn Ldr Don Gordon's No 402 Sqn from No 127 Wing found some He 115 floatplanes moored at Ribnetz, and during a series of strafing runs they destroyed one of them and damaged a second. Gordon led his men back here the following morning, and the ten-victory ace destroyed another floatplane to record his first claim with the Spitfire XIV. He described the attack in his Combat Report;

'There were six floatplanes moored on the water. My section went in on the deck. I selected the centre He 115 of the three moored in line abreast and fired a three-second burst, closing from 800 yards to 200 yards. It caught fire, and when I left, smoke from this aircraft had risen to 500 ft.'

It was not all one-way traffic on the 27th, however, as Australian pilot Wt Off A D Miller of No 130 Sqn was hit and killed by return fire from a Ju 188 that he was attacking near Wismar.

THE LAST RITES

In spite of all the problems it faced, the Luftwaffe continued to send out fighters on ground attack and intercept sorties, and larger aircraft were also seen evacuating areas under threat, especially in the east. One such machine was an He 111 found by No 41 Sqn in the late afternoon of 28 April. Shortly after 1700 hrs, Plt Off Pat Coleman, in MV264/EB-Q, and his section (Wt Offs Chalmers and Hale and Flt Sgt Moyle) were scrambled, and he later described what happened in his Combat Report;

'After attacking and blowing up a 15cwt truck at Mestlin, I reformed the section to proceed northwards, at which point I sighted a low-flying He 111 with green camouflage and the usual markings. I went into attack, ordering the rest of the section to follow. I fired a long burst with 20 degrees deflection, observing strikes on its wings and fuselage, from 400 yards closing to 200 yards. I saw the rear gunner, who had been firing at me, cease abruptly after scoring one hit on my port wing. I broke left.'

The other three Spitfires then attacked in turn, ending with the Heinkel crash-landing in flames. The four pilots were each credited with a share in the demise of the hapless bomber.

Several hours later, Flt Lt Tony Gaze led a section of No 41 Sqn on an armed reconnaissance sweep that initially started at an altitude of about 8000 ft. Some 50 minutes after taking off, he spotted enemy activity around Schwerin airfield. A somewhat confused combat ensued and he made a claim, with which he was clearly not happy, as he recounted later;

No 41 Sqn's Spitfire XIV MV264/ EB-Q was flown by Plt Off Pat Coleman on the afternoon of 28 April 1945 when his section shot down an lone He 111. His share in this kill brought him his fourth victory (*via M J F Bowyer*)

'I identified the aircraft as definitely being Fw 190s, and attacked one of a pair climbing towards us. My gunsight was unserviceable, so I closed to about 150 yards before opening fire, and the '190 half-rolled away just as I fired. I overshot and turned to follow it down, but saw "Blue 2" chasing it so I went for his pal instead. As I broke through the cloud, I saw an aircraft hit the deck and burn near the marshalling yards north of the aerodrome. I thought that this was "Blue 2", who had called up to say he was hit, but as we all returned safely, this must have been a Hun. "Blue 3" and "4" do not want to claim this so there is nothing left but for myself and "Blue 2" (Flt Lt Wilkinson) to claim it shared.

'Immediately after this attack the cloud covered the aerodrome, so we returned to base. I saw "Blue 2's" '190 explode about 50 yards in front of him and the pieces fall on the aerodrome.'

With one and a shared victory, John Wilkinson had thus became an ace in less than a fortnight, whilst Gaze's share made him a Griffon Spitfire ace too.

On 29 April the Elbe was forced with relatively little opposition in the vicinity of Lauenburg. Now the push toward the Baltic coast, and a link up with Soviet forces advancing from the east, began in earnest. As the massive assaults from east and west began to close in on the remaining enemy territory, the final demise of the Luftwaffe and the virtual destruction of its remaining effective units was now only days away. For the Griffon Spitfire units, this final phase of the war was to see one last sustained period of action and success – and the creation of a number of new aces.

30 April would prove to be a particularly successful day for the Spitfire XIV units, and No 130 Sqn in particular. It mounted some 30 sorties, including a sweep at 0945 hrs during which Canadian Flt Lt Bill Stowe shot down an Fw 190 and shared a second with Flg Off Trevorrow. Theses successes made him an ace, while Flg Off Geoff Lord claimed another during the same engagement to notch up his second kill.

An hour later four Spitfire XIVs from No 350 Sqn were patrolling in the Wittenberg area when they ran into 20 Fw 190s near Lake Schwerin as the latter were preparing to land. V1 ace Flt Lt Pat Bangerter shot down two to claim his first successes against aircraft, Plt Off Des Watkins also downed a pair and destroyed another on the ground, while Flt Sgt Guy Gigot destroyed a fifth – all three pilots also shared in the destruction of a sixth Fw 190. The unfortunate Focke-Wulfs were probably from I.(Pz)/SG 9, which was returning from an attack on advancing Allied armour. Among those lost were three holders of the Knight's Cross.

At 1130 hrs, a section of No 130 Sqn aircraft started scouring the Lake Schwerin area and quickly spotted another group of Fw 190s. In yet another one-sided fight, Flt Lt Ian Ponsford reached ace status in spectacular style when he downed two Fw 190s and shared in the destruction of two more to take his tally to six and two shared destroyed. The latter were split with experienced Australian pilot Freddie Edwards, who also destroyed an Fw 190, as he described in his Combat Report;

'We were airborne on a patrol, and when at 4000 ft I spotted about a dozen Fw 190s in the circuit of a landing ground south of the lake at Schwerin. I went down and made a head-on attack on one of them, opening fire from about 400 yards and closing to 200 yards. I did not see

On 30 April 1945 Flt Lt Ian Ponsford became an ace in spectacular style when he shot down a brace of Fw 190s and shared in the destruction of a further pair (*via C H Thomas*)

any strikes. I pulled away, turned to port and got on the tail of another aircraft and fired at it from a 45-degree angle off, reducing to about 15 degrees. Again I did not see any strikes, but almost at once my "No 1", who had not yet attacked, called up to say that one of the aircraft I had attacked had gone down and exploded on the ground.'

In the midst of the fight a patrol from No 402 Sqn arrived on the scene, and its pilots claimed another six Fw 190s and a passing Ju 88! The Canadian unit gained further successes during a follow-up patrol conducted later that afternoon, as did No 130 Sqn CO Sqn Ldr Frank Woolley, who shot down yet another Fw 190 near Winsen. Further patrols were flown in this area well into the evening, and Flt Sgt Brian Woodman continued his run of success by shooting down another somewhat helpless Si 204. Finally, Sqn Ldr John Shepherd of No 41 Sqn was successful once again during a defensive patrol over the Elbe bridgehead, as he recorded in his Combat Report;

'I saw an Fw 190 bomber slightly above and at "12 o'clock", coming towards me. I pulled up and around onto his tail as he passed and gave him a short burst – he immediately caught fire and crashed in flames. He jettisoned his cockpit hood, but no pilot appeared to get out. Returning to the bridgehead, an Me 109 appeared through cloud. I chased and opened fire from approximately 400 yards, obtaining strikes and causing a thick trail of Glycol smoke to pour from underneath. He immediately jettisoned his hood and dived for the deck. I followed, giving him about three more short bursts and getting strikes each time. He finally crash-landed heavily in a field. I gave him another burst on the ground, causing the wreckage to catch fire. No one appeared to get out of the wreck.'

During this same action, Shepherd's 'A' Flight commander, Flt Lt Tony Gaze, claimed his final success when he downed an Fw 190D-9 to take his final total to 11 and three shared victories.

Although not known by the Allies at the time, the end of the war in Europe was near. Trapped in his bunker in Berlin, Adolf Hitler had committed suicide and the seat of the Nazi regime had moved to Schleswig-Holstein – directly in the path of the advancing British Army.

Among the four Spitfire victories claimed by Flt Lt Peter Cowell of No 41 Sqn was an Me 262. His final claims were a pair of Fw 190s that he destroyed in the Lake Schwerin area on 1 May 1945 (*P Cowell via C F Shores*)

FINAL ACES

As May dawned, patrols continued over the bridgehead, and at lunchtime on the 1st a No 41 Sqn section led by Flt Lt Peter Cowell was in action when they ran into a formation of Fw 190D-9s from 13./JG 51. These aircraft, led by Fähnrich Oberfeldwebel Heinz Marquard (a 121-victory Eastern Front *experte*), were escorting ground attack Fw 190Fs on what was to be their final mission before surrendering! As they approached Schwerin, they were engaged by the No 41 Sqn formation, and in the short but fierce battle which followed, Peter Cowell brought down one of the enemy aircraft;

'I attacked the Fw 190 flying on the starboard side, opening fire at about 300 yards. Strikes were observed and the aircraft streamed smoke and pulled up almost vertically.'

Cowell then closed and fired again, sending it spinning to destruction. Although injured, the 22-year-old Marquard was fortunate enough to bail out and land in the grounds of a hospital. Cowell then spotted another fighter. 'I attacked him, opening fire at 300 yards. A large piece

Flg Off Pat Coleman was credited with seven victories while flying Spitfire XIVs with No 41 Sqn during the final weeks of the war. He reached ace status on 1 May when he shot down three Fw 190s in a single sortie (*via C H Thomas*)

Australian Flg Off Eric Gray of No 41 Sqn poses near the tail of the Spitfire XIV in which he claimed his fourth, and final, victory – an Fw 190 that he shared with his CO, Sqn Ldr Shepherd – on 1 May. This was also Shepherd's final success (*via M J F Bowyer*)

flew off his port wing and the pilot bailed out'. A third aircraft was also destroyed by the section, with two more being damaged.

Several hours later No 130 Sqn had a brief engagement, during which Flg Off Geoff Lord claimed another victory. Then it was No 350 Sqn's turn, its pilots claiming four more Fw 190s in the Lake Schwerin area. Finally, shortly after dusk, No 41 Sqn's Plt Off Pat Coleman was involved in a remarkable combat from which he emerged as an ace. Having become separated from his section in the failing light, he continued alone along the Baltic coast, before eventually heading home. As he approached Witteburg, Coleman spotted a group of Fw 190s;

'I climbed to attack the rearmost of the gaggle, but found the two leaders on my tail firing at me. I evaded the foremost in a climbing turn through the cloud, then swiftly descended again and found only one Fw in view. I attacked this one using the gyro sight, but he climbed and my gyro sight disappeared below my vision, however. I continued to pull my nose straight through him whilst firing, and observed strikes about the cockpit.

'The aircraft went into a tight spiral towards the ground, but I didn't attempt to follow up my attack until I saw it straighten out on an easterly course. I then pursued, closing rapidly, saw the pilot jettison his hood, losing height all the time, and finally bail out – I believe too low for his parachute to open fully. The aircraft crashed in flames, and I observed the pilot, a motionless figure on the ground beside his 'chute.'

On 2 May 1945 no fewer than five Griffon Spitfire pilots achieved ace status, with the first of them being Yorkshireman Flg Off Geoff Lord of No 130 Sqn, who shot down 2.5 Bu 131 trainers (*via C H Thomas*)

Continuing down to the Lake Schwerin area, Coleman was attacked by a long-nosed Fw 190D-9 and dived away, spotting a pair of aircraft over the water;

'I continued my dive towards them and recognised the aircraft as Fw 190s. Preparing to fire at 800 yards behind them, I saw the left hand fighter turn sharply into the other. The two aircraft interlocked and plunged into the northerly waters of the lake, the cause, presumably, panic.'

He was credited with three destroyed. The rest of the formation had also engaged the enemy during the sweep, and John Shepherd shared another Fw 190 with Flg Off Eric Gray – this was the former's final claim. In an amazing two weeks with the squadron, Shepherd had been credited with six and two shared victories, taking his final total to eight and five shared kills.

More was to follow on 2 May, which for the Spitfire XIV squadrons became 'the day of the aces', as no fewer than five pilots attained this much-coveted status – and a V1 ace claimed his fourth aerial kill too. Despite the last rites of the Third Reich being conducted, Allied air activity continued unabated both in support of ground forces and in an attempt to stop the increasing number of enemy aircraft trying to flee Germany for Denmark and Norway.

No 130 Sqn had sent out a patrol from Celle soon after dawn, and at 0615 hrs near Schwerin Lake they found a formation of five Bucker Bu 131 trainers – a somewhat odd type to meet in the combat area. In the ensuing very one-sided fight, both Flg Off Geoff Lord and Flt Sgt Brian Woodman each claimed their fifth victories to become aces. Lord shot down two and Woodman a third, before the pair shared a fourth. These were to be the last victories for both pilots, and they were each awarded DFCs several months later. The citation accompanying Woodman's medal noted;

'This warrant officer has destroyed or damaged at least 58 of the enemy's mechanical transport vehicles. He has taken the fullest advantage of every opportunity to engage the enemy both in the air and on the ground, and the results which he has achieved have been outstanding.'

Then, in the same area, a little before 0900 hrs, Plt Off Freddie Edwards reached acedom when, in the company of Flg Off Mertens, he shared in the destruction of a Bf 109.

The tactical reconnaissance units also reaped this rich harvest of targets when, soon after lunchtime, Flt Lt 'Sammy' Hall (who already had three victories to his name) from No 414 Sqn appeared over Neustadt/Gleve airfield and in a trice had reached acedom when he shot down three Fw 190s and a hapless Bf 108 liaison aircraft. He also damaged one of each type for good measure too! This remarkable action in which he made six claims was recounted in his Combat Report;

'I was on a tactical reconnaissance mission which I was unable to complete owing to weather. I lost my "No 2" in the cloud and instructed him to return to base. I went below the cloud, and while flying west at zero feet at 1310 hrs I sighted one Fw 190 flying north at 50 ft. I broke to starboard and rapidly closed on its tail. I opened fire at 250 yards, using approximately 25 degrees port deflection, and closed to 100 yards. I saw strikes on the fuselage and the aircraft went straight in.

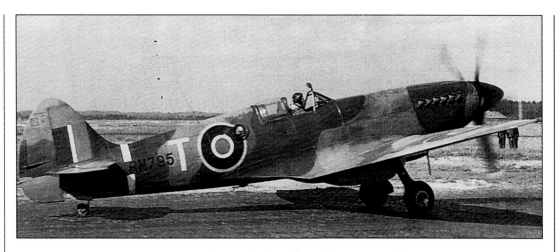

The tactical reconnaissance pilots of No 414 Sqn claimed several successes on 2 May 1945, including the four victories credited to Flt Lt 'Sammy' Hall which made him an ace. Included in the squadron's roster of aircraft at this time was RM795/T (*via M J F Bowyer*)

'Immediately in front of me I saw another Fw 190, which I overtook very rapidly and obtained only a short burst, opening fire at 50 yards. I saw strikes on the aircraft, but was unable to observe the results due to the speed at which I passed him. A further Fw 190 was immediately ahead, and I opened fire at 200 yards and closed to 50 yards. I saw strikes and flames and then observed its port wing falling off.

'Once again there was another Fw 190 immediately in line, and I opened fire at 200 yards, closing to 100 yards. I saw strikes on the aircraft, which broke to port, began to pour smoke and then burst into flames. I then broke to starboard and saw two Me 108s flying south, line abreast, at an altitude of approximately 50 ft. One broke to starboard and the other to port. I closed on the one that had broken to starboard, opening fire at 200 yards before I overshot – I obtained strikes on the aircraft. He continued to break to starboard and I broke to port and closed on the other Me 108. I opened fire at 200 yards, closing to 50 yards. I saw strikes and the aircraft exploded when it hit the ground.'

Shortly after Hall had completed possibly the most outstanding solo feat of airmanship in a Griffon Spitfire, his CO, Sqn Ldr Jim Prendergast, shot down two more Fw 190s over Wismar harbour to claim his only victories. 'Sammy' Hall received a bar to his DFC for his exploits on this day.

However, the Spitfires did not have it all their own way on the 2nd, for whilst strafing trucks in the late afternoon the aircraft flown by No 130 Sqn's Flt Lt Bill Stowe, who had become an ace a few days earlier, was hit by debris and the pilot forced to crash-land near Lake Schwerin.

A short while later, at 1710 hrs, six aircraft from No 350 Sqn up on an armed reconnaissance sweep of the Schlewig-Holstein area sighted an Ar 234 on the approach to Hohn airfield. Four Spitfires attacked the

'Sammy' Hall's CO at No 414 Sqn was Sqn Ldr Jim Prendergast, who also enjoyed success on 2 May 1945 when he downed two Fw 190s to register his only victories of the war (*via L Milberry*)

Spitfire RB155/MN-C also saw action on 2 May 1945 when Flt Sgt Andre Kicq used it to help destroy an Ar 234 for No 350 Sqn's final victory of the war. Twelve days earlier, Plt Off Des Watkins had claimed the first of his five victories with the aircraft (*G L Watkins*)

The last pilot to become an ace flying a Griffon Spitfire was Plt Off Desmond Watkins of No 350 Sqn, whose share of the Ar 234 destroyed on 2 May 1945 was his fifth success (*G L Watkins*)

jet bomber and shot it down, the Arado's demise being shared between Flt Lt Bangerter, Flg Off Van Eeckhoudt, Plt Off Des Watkins and Flt Sgt Andre Kicq. The destruction of Oberleutnant Worzech's Ar 234 4U+EH of 1(F)./123 was No 350 Sqn's final aerial victory of the war, and it also made Watkins an ace. He was the last pilot to reach this status on the Griffon Spitfire. Watkins stated in his Combat Report;

'At about 1710 hrs, whilst flying at 8000 ft, I saw in the circuit of Hohn aerodrome a jet aircraft which I identified as an Arado 234 going in to land. I dived from 8000 ft, followed by the rest of the section, closed to within 50 yards behind the aircraft and sprayed the mainplane and side of fuselage with machine gun fire. I broke away to port as soon as I saw that the aircraft was smoking.'

Bangerter then attacked and obtained hits on the Ar 234's port wing root and engine, which burst into flames. He was followed by the other two pilots in the section, and their combined fire caused the jet to flip over onto its back and shed its port wing, before finally crashing in a ball of fire. The section then pressed on with its mission, subsequently shooting up a locomotive and some vehicles. Watkins also received the DFC shortly after VE-Day, his citation stating that 'He has at all times set a high example to his fellow pilots'.

FINALE

In spite of the clearly hopeless situation, German resistance continued, as did Allied air attacks. No 125 Wing's operations diary for 3 May baldly recorded;

'With the enemy pocket shrinking rapidly, great care had to be exercised before any ground targets could be attacked. We started off with a highly successful attack by No 350 Sqn on a column of 40+ vehicles on the road between Lubeck and Kiel. Twenty vehicles were destroyed, and from the way they burned, they appeared to be laden with petrol. Before breakfast Flg Off Trevorrow and Plt Off Edwards of No 130 Sqn destroyed a Ju 188.'

This shared victory took No 130 Sqn's ebullient Freddie Edwards' final score to six. For No 41 Sqn an even more significant event beckoned that

No 41 Sqn flew Spitfires throughout World War 2, and its 200th, and final, victory was claimed by this aircraft – NH915/EB-H – when in the hands of Flt Lt Derek Rake. The latter is seen here posing with the fighter shortly after achieving this milestone with the destruction of a Ju 188 on 3 May (*D S V Rake*)

day. Having flown Spitfires for the entire war, the unit had taken its total to a tantalising 199 aircraft destroyed and there was much speculation as to whether they could achieve the 'double ton' before the imminent ceasefire. They did, as Flt Lt Derek Rake recalled to the author especially for this volume;

'You can probably imagine the enthusiasm within the whole of the squadron to search and destroy the 200th enemy aircraft – but they were becoming very difficult to find by early May 1945!

'It so happened that on the 3rd, I was leading a flight in the Lubeck-Keil area in my favourite Spitfire "EB-H" when we spotted a Ju 188. He saw us at about the same time, and dived for the deck. I got on his tail, but he was flying so low that I could not get a bead on him until he had to pull up over some trees. A short burst was enough and he crash-landed a few hundred yards further on. That was the 200th kill for No 41 Sqn.

'My upward victory roll upon our return to Celle was not appreciated by our Airfield Commander, Gp Capt J E Johnson. The "rocket" was deserved!'

By the end of hostilities, No 41 Sqn had been credited with destroying exactly 200 enemy aircraft, probably destroying 61 and damaging 109, as

No 402 Sqn completed its final wartime sortie on 5 May 1945 when its CO, 'Chunky' Gordon, flew a Mk XIV alongside Merlin Spitfires piloted by the other squadron COs of No 126 Wing. This photograph of MV310/AE-C was taken at B116 Wunstorf on that very day (*via C H Thomas*)

well as bringing down 53 V1s. These successes had cost the unit 64 pilots killed and 21 as PoWs.

Soon after 1030 hrs on 3 May – two hours after No 41 Sqn's notable achievement – the Canadians of No 402 Sqn were out patrolling near Neumunster when they spotted a number of Fi 156s on the ground. Flt Lts Innes and Peck had damaged three of them when another was seen in the air. Their CO, Sqn Ldr Don Gordon, recounted;

'At 4000 ft west of Neumunster, my No 2 reported an aircraft flying near the deck. He went down and made an attack on it, identifying his target as a Fieseler Storch. He missed it completely, so I followed him in and opened fire at 400 yards, with 90 degrees deflection, seeing strikes all over the aircraft. It caught fire in the air and crashed in flames.'

The tiny spotter aircraft was the last victory claimed by an ace while flying a Griffon Spitfire.

This was almost the final act in northwest Germany, as the No 127 Wing record book for 4 May lamented;

'Today, with poor weather and a battleground nearly out of reach, we could hope for little spectacular. A strong crosswind developed in the afternoon and operations ended early.'

That evening, all the enemy forces in the 21st Army Group area surrendered unconditionally, although there remained some resistance on the eastern front. One of the provisions of the surrender was a complete ban of any flying by the Luftwaffe, but so desperate was the desire to escape the Soviets that some sorties were made.

Early on the 5th a patrol from No 130 Sqn spotted an Si 204 over the sea off Hamburg, and when it started evasive action it was shot down by Flt Lt Gibbons and Wt Off Seymour. This Siebel transport aircraft duly become the last victim of the war to fall to a Spitfire XIV, and it was also the last victory claimed by the 2nd TAF. Soon afterwards the section spotted four Fw 190s, but the pilots in these aircraft promptly lowered their undercarriages and waggled their wings, and as soon as they approached the British strip at Fassburg (B152) they landed.

Soon afterwards Flt Lt Derek Rake led No 41 Sqn's final war patrol, which returned to base at 0800 hrs. A short while later No 350 Sqn also

When No 41 Sqn moved up to Denmark on 9 May 1945, MV260/EB-P became the aircraft of Flt Lt Tony Gaze. Prior to that, it had been flown by a number of No 41 Sqn's most notable late-war pilots, including John Wilkinson, Peter Cowell and Bill Stowe (*W N Stowe via C H Thomas*)

As the war ended, veteran No 401 Sqn was in the final throes of converting to Griffon Spitfires. Tragically, its CO, 15-victory ace Sqn Ldr Bill Klersy, was killed in an accident flying one of them on 22 May 1945 (*Canadian Forces*)

After the end of the war the RAAF briefly retained some units in Europe for occupation duties, including Spitfire FR XIV-equipped No 451 Sqn (*P R Arnold collection*)

flew its last patrol too. The Canadians in No 126 Wing marked their final sorties with a formation made of Spitfires flown by the squadron commanders and led by Wing Leader Wg Cdr Geoff Northcott. The formation consisted entirely of Spitfire IXs, bar the solitary Mk XIV flown by Sqn Ldr Gordon of No 402 Sqn. The wing's diary noted;

'They looked everywhere for the "damned elusive Hun" for 1 hour and 45 minutes, but having enjoyed no luck, they landed at Wunstorf at 0800 hrs, thus ending "the last patrol".'

The surrender led to a need to disarm the enemy throughout the area, and on the 9th No 41 Sqn was moved up to B160 at Kastrup, in Denmark. A few days earlier No 401 Sqn had at last completed its transition to Mk XIVs. However, the unit's diary entry for 22 May sombrely recorded the passing of another ace;

'A very heavy blow was dealt to the squadron today when the CO, Sqn Ldr W T Klersy DFC and Bar, who has so ably led the squadron for the past five months, was reported missing on a training flight. He was leading a flight of three aircraft when they ran into cloud and he was seen to make a fast turn in the cloud.'

Sadly, three days later, his body was found in the burned out wreckage of his Spitfire XIV near Wesel where it had crashed.

The last Griffon Spitfire operations were flown from the UK on 12 May when No 1 Sqn, under the command of V1 ace and successful Griffon Spitfire pilot Sqn Ldr Ray Nash, having re-equipped with Spitfire XXIs, flew its first, and only, operation as the unit's record book entry described. 'Shortly after lunch Sqn Ldr Nash led the unit to Warmwell for operations over the Channel Islands'. The Spitfire's last operation in Europe went ahead the next day;

'At 0725 hrs they were airborne from Warmwell and flew over the Channel Islands, whilst the Navy made its official landing to take over. No undue excitement was seen, and the unit landed back at 0915 hrs.'

The Spitfire XIV had proved to be a superb weapon in the heavy air fighting during the campaign in Western Europe, and had achieved a real ascendancy over the enemy. No less a figure than the former Inspector General of the Luftwaffe General Adolf Galland recorded a highly appropriate epitaph to the type when he wrote, 'The best thing about the Spitfire Mk XIV was that there were so few of them'.

A KIND OF PEACE

The German surrender found the bulk of the 2nd TAF based north of a line dissecting Bremen, Hamburg and Kiel, and in the succeeding weeks it rapidly began to transform from a tactical formation into one of occupation. As the disarming of surrendering enemy forces commenced in earnest, the Spitfire XIV units of No 125 Wing, led by Gp Capt Johnnie Johnson, moved north to Denmark and established themselves at B160 Kastrup, near Copenhagen.

The post-war rundown soon began to bite, however, and on 15 July 2nd TAF was restyled as the British Air Forces of Occupation (BAFO), whose establishment boasted a number of Spitfire XIV squadrons, including, briefly, the RAAF's Nos 451 and 453 Sqns. Also remaining were those of the Canadian No 126 Wing, which was led by nine-victory ace Wg Cdr Geoff Northcott. Nos 411, 412, 416 and 443 Sqns also converted to Spitfire XIVs as part of the BAFO, and they continued to fly these until all four units were withdrawn the following spring.

Another wing commanded by a wartime ace was No 123 at Wunstorf, which controlled Spitfire XIV-equipped No 41 (later re-numbered 26) Sqn. It was led by the RAF's top Typhoon ace, with 16 victories, Gp Capt Johnny Baldwin, who also flew a personally-marked Spitfire.

Fighter units in BAFO gradually switched to Tempests, while Fighter Command's Griffon Spitfire squadrons soon replaced their aircraft with

By the autumn of 1945 the Canadian No 126 Wing at Utersen was led by nine-victory ace Wg Cdr G W Northcott (*Canadian Forces*)

A number of RCAF squadrons quickly re-equipped with Spitfire XIVs for service with BAFO post-war, among them No 416 Sqn, led by 11-victory ace Sqn Ldr John Mitchner. One of its aircraft was TZ112/DN-Y (*via C G Jefford*)

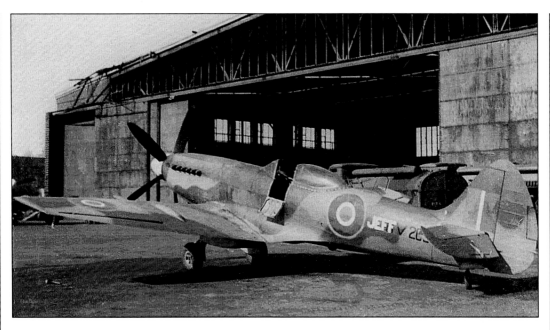

No 126 Wing leader Wg Cdr Geoff Northcott flew this personally-marked Spitfire XIV MV263/JEFF post-war (*via C G Jefford*)

The CO of No 123 Wing after the war was Typhoon ace Gp Capt Johnny Baldwin, who had his initials painted on the nose of his personal Spitfire XIV (*P H T Green collection*)

Meteor and Vampire jets. They in turn passed on their piston-engined fighters to the Auxiliary squadrons that were reforming.

No 80 Sqn remained Spitfire equipped into 1948, however, with the Wunstorf-based unit being commanded by successful wartime Mk XIV pilot Sqn Ldr Dickie Newbery. In January of that year the squadron began re-equipping with the ultimate Spitfire – the F 24. With tensions growing between the western Allies and the Soviet Bloc over the control of Berlin, the squadron was quickly moved to Gatow to provide ground units with additional support in the divided city. It eventually returned to more normal duties later in the year.

Although Griffon Spitfires remained with some reconnaissance units, amongst whose number were several ace pilots, No 80 Sqn was the last in the fighter role in BAFO, and it left for Hong Kong in mid-1949.

THE LAST VICTORIES

Palestine, which was controlled by Britain under a League of Nations mandate, had seen considerable violence between its Arab and Jewish inhabitants between the wars, and the influx of stateless Jews following the end of World War 2 increased tensions between the communities. This was further exacerbated by the desire for a Jewish state, and led to clashes with British forces.

Among the RAF units based in Palestine for air policing were two squadrons flying Griffon engined Spitfire FR 18s, the first of which were received in August 1946 by No 208 Sqn at Ein Shemer. On 15 May 1947, the squadron came under the command of Sqn Ldr Charles Ambrose, who had a total of eight claims (two and one shared destroyed, four probables and one damaged). The following month No 32 Sqn, based at Ramat David, outside Haifa, began replacing its Spitfire IXs with FR 18s. It was commanded by Sqn Ldr Arthur Todd, who had three victories to his name, including one of the very few to be claimed by the RAF over West Africa.

The Spitfires of both units were kept busy with patrols that ensured the convoy routes were kept clear of obstructions left by local terrorist groups, and more offensive actions were also flown when the need arose.

In preparation for the complete British withdrawal after the creation of the State of Israel, both squadrons moved to Nicosia, on Cyprus, at the end of March 1948, although they maintained detachments at Ramat David to continue their policing patrols. And it was from here in April that they supported an attack by armoured cars from the Life Guards and 4/7 Dragoon Guards against a Jewish headquarters in Jaffa, where the militia were frustrating efforts to evacuate the port.

After the war several aces continued to fly Spitfires, including Polish pilot Wt Off Miroslaw Wojciechowski, who performed photo-reconnaissance duties with No 2 Sqn in BAFO – he regularly flew PR 19 PM627/OI-X during this period (R C B Ashworth)

Two units equipped with Spitfire FR 18s, including No 32 Sqn, to which TP330/GZ-G belonged, were based in Palestine for policing duties post-war (*No 32 Sqn Records*)

Spitfire FR 18 TZ240/RG-A of No 208 Sqn taxis out for another policing patrol from Ein Shemer in 1948, when the unit was heavily engaged in supporting ground forces (*author's collection*)

When the new State was created on 14 May, it immediately came under attack from neighbouring Arab countries, and heavy fighting resulted. Some British units remained temporarily based in Israel to cover the final withdrawal, and these occasionally became embroiled with the protagonists.

There had been air action involving both sides, but soon after dawn on 22 May two Royal Egyptian Air Force (REAF) Spitfires attacked – possibly in error – the RAF Spitfire detachment that was neatly lined up at Ramat David, leaving two fighters destroyed and damaging eight others to varying degrees. When the Egyptian Spitfires returned a little over an hour later, they hit a landing Dakota, killing several of its crew, and destroyed a second aircraft, before the standing RAF Spitfire patrol of Flg Offs Geoff Cooper and Roy Bowie from No 208 Sqn were ordered to engage. Bowie subsequently recalled his attack on the Spitfire of Sqn Ldr Nasr al Din in his Combat Report;

'We dived in over the airfield and intercepted a Spitfire with Egyptian markings. We spoke to Sqn Ldr Ambrose, who told us to shoot him down

During the various skirmishes with the Egyptians and the Israelis in 1948-49, Flg Off Tim McElhaw was credited with two Spitfires destroyed. However, on 7 January 1949, he was flying one of two No 208 Sqn Spitfire FR 18s shot down by former RCAF ace John McElroy, who was flying a Spitfire IX of the Israeli Defence Force Air Force's No 101 Sqn. McElhaw bailed out and was held captive by the Israelis for a short time (*T McElhaw*)

The first fighters based at Kai Tak, in Hong Kong, after the war were the Spitfire XIVs of No 132 Sqn. RN133/FF-B belonged to the CO, Sqn Ldr Ken Charney, and was named *Jean VI* (*via J D R Rawlings*)

– which we did – whereupon another Spitfire appeared, which we chased at ground level off to the south. Geoff got in several bursts, which raised a great deal of dirt, and the last one hit fair and square and the aircraft disappeared in a cloud of dust.'

A third Spitfire, flown by Flg Off Abd al Rahman Inan, was shot down by ground fire.

Two hours later, the REAF attacked for a third time, and the standing patrol being mounted by Flg Offs McElhaw and Hully intercepted the raid. Tim McElhaw, who was flying TZ228, later recounted;

'I saw a single Spitfire turning over the airfield and came in behind it. It had clear Egyptian markings, and terrified of precipitating a diplomatic incident, I called the tower asking if I could shoot it down. The CO said something like "Yes, get him".

'Meanwhile, his chum dived for the deck and nipped up a narrow valley in the hills at about 15 ft, hoping to lose me I suppose. Well, my excess speed was so great that I had to cut the throttle to avoid overtaking him. I gave him three short bursts from close up, and he just went straight in. It was the first time that I had done any air-to-air firing. I had barely completed the turn over the airfield when I saw another. Les took a pot at him and then I put in a longish burst. Some bits came off and down he went – he made a good prang when he hit the ground, as he still had one bomb on!'

The Egyptians' costly mistake had virtually wiped out the REAF's No 2 Sqn, and the following day the remaining flyable RAF Spitfires thankfully withdrew to Cyprus, where No 32 Sqn was re-equipped with Vampires in July. On the 8th of that month Charles Ambrose was succeeded as No 208 Sqn CO by 7.5-victory ace Sqn Ldr John Morgan, who in November led the squadron to Fayid, on the Suez Canal.

By that time hostilities between Israel and Egypt had flared up once again, and the Israelis had pushed into Sinai, resulting in the RAF flying regular reconnaissance sorties from Fayid to monitor the fighting.

On the 7 January 1949, No 208 Sqn was ordered to fly a further reconnaissance mission to clarify the situation in northeast Sinai, so just

No 132 Sqn's CO at Kai Tak was six-victory Spitfire ace Sqn Ldr Keith Charney, who had gained all his victories over Malta and France. He had been given command of No 132 Sqn in July 1944 (*ww2images*)

Among the Spitfire XIV units performing policing duties in the Far East was No 273 Sqn, which was based in Saigon supporting the re-occupation of Indo-China by French forces. RN218, flown by Sqn Ldr Hibbert, is seen here on 30 December 1945 whilst escorting the aircraft of Sir Keith Park (*A V Skeet*)

before midday four Spitfires set out. Approaching an Israeli column, the lower section of Spitfires, probably having been misidentified as Egyptian, were fired upon and both aircraft were hit. Plt Off Close was forced to bail out, while the second aircraft managed to climb away. Then two Israeli Defence Force Air Force Spitfire IXs of No 101 Sqn, one of which was flown by wartime Canadian Spitfire ace John McElroy, appeared and attacked the covering pair. The latter's accurate fire made short work of the remaining No 208 Sqn aircraft, taking McElroy's final tally to 16. Plt Off R Sayers (in TZ228) was killed and Flg Off Tim McElhaw (flying TP456) was forced to bail out.

Meanwhile, the other Israeli aircraft, flown by 'Slick' Goodwin, chased down the one remaining, damaged, Spitfire FR 18, and eventually Flg Off Cooper was hit and wounded, and also forced to abandon his aircraft. He was picked up by Bedouin and eventually returned, but the Israelis imprisoned McElhaw and Close.

Several hours later, a patrol of Tempests and Spitfires searching for the earlier aircraft also had a skirmish with the Israelis over Sinai, resulting in the loss of a Tempest and its pilot and damage to others. In spite of these losses no retaliation was authorised.

It is a particular irony, therefore, that the RAF's final Spitfire victories and losses in air combat should have been claimed over, or inflicted by, other Spitfires!

FAR EAST POLICING

As production of the Mk XIV increased, in January 1945 shipments of Griffon Spitfires began to be sent to India in an effort to re-equip squadrons fighting the Japanese in Burma. Led by six-victory ace Sqn Ldr Ken Charney, No 132 Sqn had moved to Ceylon in early 1945 and then on to Madura, in southern India, in May, where it became the first in-theatre to convert to the Spitfire XIV. The following month two more Spitfire VIII units arrived at Madura for re-equipment. No 17 Sqn was led by Battle of Britain ace Sqn Ldr 'Ginger' Lacey, while No 11 Sqn was commanded by Sqn Ldr B T Shannon. Flying with No 17 Sqn at the time was Flt Lt Don Healey, who recalled the arrival of the new aircraft;

'We didn't get off to a great start with the Spitfire XIVE, as the first one that arrived at Madura had the latest cutback fuselage, which drew the retort "this isn't a bloody Spitfire" from our somewhat maverick CO, Sqn Ldr 'Ginger' Lacey, who promptly had them passed on to No 11 Sqn! He refused to budge, and eventually high back aircraft were flown in for No 17 Sqn.'

The squadrons began working up for the invasion of Malaya, but the sudden end to the war with Japan meant they became part of the re-occupation force for Britain's Far East territories instead. No 132 Sqn was embarked in HMS *Smiter* in early September and sailed for Hong Kong, where it set up base at Kai Tak until disbandment the following April. The other two squadrons, Nos 11 and 17, were embarked in HMS *Trumpeter,* and after somewhat precariously flying off the aircraft carrier, they had become settled at Seletar, in Singapore, by month-end. Both units then moved on to Kuala Lumpur the following January.

Elsewhere, by the end of the year No 20 Sqn was at Don Muang, near Bangkok, and No 273 Sqn was flying out of Tan Son Nhut, Saigon, where in late November the arrival of the magnificently moustachioed Sqn Ldr W J Hibbert coincided with the delivery of bubble-hooded Spitfire XIVs. The unit had been flying covering patrols as French forces encountered increasing resistance from local nationalists. The last of these sorties was performed on 8 January 1946 and the squadron disbanded soon afterwards.

Further south, in the Dutch East Indies, Indonesian nationalists clashed with British forces as they re-occupied the area pending renewal of Dutch rule, and in December 1945 No 155 Sqn was allocated six Spitfire XIVs, which were greeted with enthusiasm. The squadron record book recorded, 'We feel that the XIVs will be a step nearer jets'. Two months later the unit moved to Medan, in Sumatra, from where it performed policing operations until August 1946.

When the Spitfire XIVs of No 17 Sqn first moved to Japan as part of the Occupation Force in early 1946, the unit was commanded by the legendary ace Sqn Ldr 'Ginger' Lacey. RN135 was his aircraft during his tenure as CO (*D Healey*)

In April 1946, Nos 11 and 17 Sqns embarked in HMS *Vengeance*, and in early May they became established at Miho, on the Japanese east coast, as part of the British Commonwealth Occupation Force. Lacey returned to England soon afterwards, as both squadrons began a routine of policing and searching for signs of illegal movement in the shattered country. In mid-November Sqn Ldr Pat Hancock, who had made nine air combat claims (including three destroyed), assumed command of the No 17 Sqn.

The following August, the unit welcomed another wartime ace as its CO when Sqn Ldr Archie Winskill (who had six victories) arrived in Japan, replacing Sqn Ldr F A Robinson. However, with little real need for aerial policing, both squadrons were disbanded in February 1948.

In India, No 34 Sqn, which was based at Palam, near Delhi, under Sqn Ldr D B Pearson, flew Griffon-engined Spitfire PR 19s in the photo-reconnaissance and survey roles. The unit was also involved in the interminable operations to keep the peace on the turbulent North West Frontier of India, operational sorties from a detachment at Kohat being flown over the Allahabad, Jubelipore and Peshawar areas for several months. The detachment returned to Palam on 6 October 1946, but continued to conduct operations over the North West Frontier Province until the granting of independence to India in July 1947, when the unit was disbanded and its aircraft passed on to the Royal Indian Air Force.

No 17 Sqn's final CO in Japan was also a wartime ace in the form of Sqn Ldr Archie Winskill, who remained in command until the unit was disbanded in February 1948 (*A L Winskill*)

THE FINAL ACTION

The peacetime establishment for the RAF in the Far East included several fighter units, one of which was No 60 Sqn, based at Tengah, in Singapore. In early December 1946, nightfighter ace Sqn Ldr Michael Constable-Maxwell assumed command as the squadron re-equipped with Spitfire FR 18s. The CO collected the first Spitfire after assembly at Seletar-based No 390 Maintenance Unit on 15 January 1947, and No 60 Sqn gradually built up to strength and began flying exercises and bomber affiliation sorties. Constable-Maxwell commented;

'Once we got our aircraft into service, life improved for us all. We loved our Spitfires, and the flying was marvellous. We had an establishment of eight aircraft, and No 28 Sqn had the same. When we were asked to give demonstrations, we usually flew as one squadron of 12 aircraft, with Broome, No 28 Sqn's CO, leading the formation while I flew round on my own. I found the best way to get a reaction from spectators was to come over the airfield as fast and low as possible, and just before I reached them, to throttle right back. This resulted in noisy explosions from the open exhausts, and as we were usually inverted at the time, people assumed things had gone wrong!'

A peacetime routine was followed, and the following July No 60 Sqn sent six aircraft to Kuala Lumpur to an army co-operation exercise. Constable-Maxwell left at the end of the year, and in April 1948 permission was given to paint individual peacetime markings on the Spitfires – No 60 Sqn displayed its first personalised aircraft at the Empire Air Day on the 22nd when it showed off its yellow and black stripes around the engine cowling.

Elsewhere, in Malaya, the local colonial administration had, since its reintroduction in 1946, been seriously threatened by the activities of the

Malayan Communist Party, who controlled a fairly large and well equipped force in the jungles of the Malay Peninsula. With acts of terrorism becoming commonplace, on 22 June 1948 a State of Emergency was declared, thus beginning the 12-year-long campaign to suppress it.

On 2 July No 60 Sqn detached three aircraft to Kuala Lumpur as part of an RAF Task Force sent to provide air support for the Army. The detachment quickly settled in, and the squadron's Spitfires flew their first strike on the 6th when they attacked a clearing near Ayer Karah, north of Ipoh. Operation *Firedog* had begun. The unit suffered several losses due to accidents in coming months during periods of varying operational intensity.

When he led the RAF's final Spitfire strike Sqn Ldr Duncan-Smith was flying his personal aircraft, NH850/Z, which was adorned with colourful black and yellow nose and spinner stripes and the No 60 Sqn badge on the fin (*via D Oliver*)

The last operational RAF Spitfire fighters were the F 24s of No 80 Sqn, based in Hong Kong. The unit flew its final 'Balbo' of five aircraft to mark the aircraft's retirement on 22 December 1951, the event being recorded for posterity in this photograph (*No 80 Sqn Records*)

From 1948, the Spitfire FR 18s of No 60 Sqn were engaged in attacks on Communist terrorists in Malaya. The aircraft's final strike with the unit was led by squadron CO, Sqn Ldr Wilf Duncan-Smith (right) – a wartime ace with 19 victories to his credit. The other pilot in this photograph is Flt Lt Jimmy James, who had flown Hurricane IICs and Spitfire VCs over Burma with No 607 Sqn in 1942-44, claiming two aircraft destroyed, one shared probably destroyed and eight damaged (*No 60 Sqn Records*)

One of the largest and most successful air strikes in the early stages of *Firedog* came on 28 February 1949 when eight Spitfires and four Beaufighters hit a group of terrorists in southern Pahang, killing nine.

In early July the CO, Sqn Ldr Broughton (received a DFC for his exploits during *Firedog*) was replaced by 19-victory World War 2 ace, Sqn Ldr W G G Duncan-Smith.

Due to the tempo of operations, and following the departure of No 28 Sqn to Hong Kong for policing work the previous year, No 60 Sqn was increased in size to 16 Spitfires, divided into two flights. On 13 October it sent 13 aircraft to Butterworth so that they could fly strikes in northern Malaya, until returning to Kuala Lumpur in early December.

Throughout the year there had been a steady increase in terrorist activity, and this continued into 1950. The squadron increased further in size with the addition of 'C' Flight, comprising three Spitfire PR 19s for reconnaissance, and these remained until November. However, the ageing Spitfires were increasingly suffering problems with serviceability, and towards the end of the year preparations were being made for No 60 Sqn to become the Far East Air Force's first jet fighter squadron, equipped with Vampires. Then, on New Year's Day 1951, Sqn Ldr Duncan-Smith (in NH850/Z) led Flg Off Walters, Flt Lt Bailey and Flg Off Keogh in a strike on a target near Kota Tinggi. This would prove to be the last operation where a Spitfire of the RAF fired its guns in anger.

This was not quite the end of operational service for Griffon-engined Spitfire fighters, however, as in mid-1949, with the civil war raging on mainland China, No 80 Sqn's Spitfire F 24s had been moved from Germany to Hong Kong to reinforce the resident No 28 Sqn. The aircraft were ferried in HMS *Ocean*, and by August the unit was established at Kai Tak. From here it began policing patrols around the colony and offshore. The Spitfires also provided increased 'presence' as tensions with Communist China markedly increased following the outbreak of the war in Korea – although No 80 Sqn's pilots viewed the prospect of combat in Spitfires against Communist MiGs with some trepidation!

In August 1951, Sqn Ldr John 'Chips' Carpenter (an eight-victory ace) became No 80 Sqn's CO, and at the end of the year the unit re-equipped with Hornets. A final Spitfire 'Balbo' was flown on 22 December, after which the last Spitfire fighters left RAF service.

The immortal words of the Bard himself, William Shakespeare, might almost have been written to mark the passing;

'Age cannot wither Her, nor custom stale Her infinite variety.'

APPENDICES

Griffon-engined Spitfire Aces

Name	Service	Unit	Griffon Claims	Total Claims	Area
Harries R H	RAF	91, Tang Wg	10?/1/-	15+3sh/2/5? & 1 V1	UK
Walmsley H E	RAF	130, 350	9+1sh/-/-	11+1sh/1/4	Eur
Ponsford R I	RAF	130	6+2sh/1/3	6+2sh/1/3	Eur
Shepherd J B	RAF	610, 41	6+2sh/-/- & 5+2sh V1	8+5sh/1?/2? & 5+2sh V1	Eur, UK
Coleman P T	RAF	41	5+2sh/-/-	5+2sh/-/-	Eur
Lord G	RAF	130	5?/-/1 & ? V1	5?/-/1 & ? V1	Eur
Gaze F A O	RAF	610, 41	4+2sh/-/- & 1 V1	11+3sh/4/5 & 1 V1	Eur
Kynaston N A	RAF	91	4?/1/1 & 22 V1	4?/1/1 & 22 V1	UK
Edwards F E F	RAAF	130	2+4sh/-/1 & ? V1	2+4sh/-/1 & ? V1	Eur
Woodman B W	RAF	130	4?/-/2	4?/-/2	Eur
Watkins D J	RAF	350	3+2sh/-/-	3+2sh/-/-	Eur
Stowe W N	RCAF	412, 130, 401, 412, 430	2+3sh/1/-	2+3sh/1/-	UK, Eur
Wilkinson J F	RAF	41	2+3sh/-/- & 1 V1	2+3sh/-/- & 1 V1	Eur

Griffon-engined Spitfire V1 Aces

Name	Service	Unit	Griffon Claims	Total Claims	Area
Balasse M A L	Belg	41	6+2sh V1	6+2sh V1	UK
Bangerter B M	RAF	610, 350	2?/-/- & 4? V1	2?/-/- & 4? V1	UK, Eur
Bond P M	RAF	91	7+3sh V1	7+3sh V1	UK
Burgwal R F	Dutch	322	19+5sh V1	19+5sh V1	UK
Collier K R	RAAF	91	7 V1	7 V1	UK
Cramm H L	Dutch	322	5 V1	5 V1	UK
Cruikshank A R	RAF	91	10? V1	10? V1	UK
de Bordas H F	FFAF	91	9? V1	9? V1	UK
Elcock A R	RAF	91	7? V1	7? V1	UK
Faulkner J A	RAF	91	4+2sh V1	1/-/- & 4+2sh V1	UK
Gibbs N P *	RCAF	41	4 V1	4 V1	UK
Janssen M J	Dutch	322	6+2sh V1	7? V1	UK
Johnson H D	RAF	91	13? V1	13? V1	UK
Jongbloed G F J	Dutch	322	7+2sh V1	1/-/1 & 8+2sh V1	UK
Jonker J	Dutch	322	5? V1	5? V1	UK
Marshall W C	RAF	91	7 V1	2/-/- & 7 V1	UK
McKinley G M	RAF	610	4? V1	4? V1	UK
McPhie R A	RCAF	91	5+3sh V1	5+3sh V1	UK
Moffett H B	RCAF	91	8 V1	8 V1	UK
Nash R S	RAF	91	2/-/- & 17+3sh V1	2?/-/1 & 17+3sh V1	UK, Eur
Neil H M	RAF	91	5 V1	5 V1	UK
Newbery R A	RAF	610	8+2sh V1	3/2/3? & 8+2sh V1	UK
Plesman J L	Dutch	322	11 V1	11 V1	UK

Spencer T	RAF	41, 350	1?/-/- & 8 V1	1?/-/- & 8 V1	UK, Eur
Topham E	RAF	91	8? V1	-/-/1 & 9? V1	UK
van Arkel J	Dutch	322	6? V1	1/-/1 & 6? V1	UK
van Beers R L	Dutch	322	5 V1	5 V1	UK
van Eedenborg C M	Dutch	322	7 V1	7 V1	UK

Griffon-engined Spitfire Aces with Over Five Claims

Name	Service	Unit	Griffon Claims	Total Claims	Area
Birbeck C R	RAF	41	2/1/2 & ? V1	2/1/2 & 2? V1	UK
Boulton J A	RAAF	130	3/2/-	3/2/-	Eur
Burrows E R	RCAF	402	1+3sh/-/2?	1+3sh/-/2?	Eur
Chalmers J A*	RAF	41	2+2sh/-/-	2+2sh/-/-	Eur
Clay P H T	RAF	130	4/-/2	4/-/2	Eur
Cowell P*	RAF	41	4/-/-	4/-/-	Eur
Gigot G F*	Belg	350	2+2sh/-/-	2+2sh/-/-	Eur
Gray E	RAAF	41	2+2sh/-/1	2+2sh/-/1	Eur
Kuhlmann K C	SAAF	322	1 V1	4/1/3 & 1 V1	Eur
Stevenson I T*	RAF	41	2/1/1 & 2? V1	2/1/1 & 2? V1	Eur
Woolley F G	RAF	41, 350, 130	4/1/-	4/1/1	Eur

Aces with some Griffon-engined Spitfire Claims

Name	Service	Unit	Griffon Claims	Total Claims	Area
Andrieux J	FFAF	91	2/2/-	6/4/2	UK
Benham D I	RAF	41	2/-/-	6+2sh/3/7	Eur
Doll J C S	RAF	91	4/-/1	4+1sh/?/1	UK
Draper D J P	RCAF	91	-/-/- & 6 V1	4+1sh/2/1 & 6 V1	UK
Glen A A	RAF	41	2/-/-	9/-/4+2sh	UK
Gordon D C	RCAF	402	1/-/- & 1 on ground	9+2sh/5/5 & 1 on ground	Eur
Hall D I	RCAF	414, 411	4/-/2	7/-/2	Eur
Keefer G C	RCAF	125 Wg	4/-/1	12/2/9	Eur
Maridor J-M*	FFAF	91	2/-/1 & 11 V1	3?/2/3 & 11 V1	UK
Oxspring R W	RAF	24 Wg	4 ? V1	13+2sh/2/12 & 4 ? V1	UK
Plinsier A M	Belg	350	1/-/-	3+3sh/1/3	UK
Samouelle C J	RAF	41, 130	3/-/2	10 ? /4/11	Eur
Schade P A	RAF	91	4? V1	13?/2/2 & 4? V1	UK
Smith D H	RAAF	41	1/-/1	5?/2/2	UK
Stenborg G	RNZAF	91	4/-/1	14?/-/3	UK

Aces who flew Griffon-engined Spitfires but made no Claims

Name	Service	Unit	Total Claims	Area
Allen H R	RAF	1	5+3sh/2?/3?	UK
Baldwin J	RAF	123 Wg	15?/-/4	Eur
Cameron G D A T	RCAF	401	5/1/3	Eur
Carpenter J M V	RAF	80	8/1/3	FE
Charney K L	RAF	132	6/4/7	FE
Charnock H W	RAF	41	8/1/-	Eur
Constable-Maxwell M H	RAF	60	6?/4/2	FE
Cook H	RAF	41	5?/-//1	UK
Dodd W G	RCAF	402	6+2sh/3/4	Eur
Duncan-Smith W G G	RAF	60	17+2sh/6+2sh/8	FE
Gray C G	RAF	Lympne Wg	27+2sh/6+4sh/12	UK
Johnson J E	RAF	125 Wg	34+7sh/3+2sh/10+3sh	Eur
Klersey W T	RCAF	401	14?/-/3	Eur
Lacey J H	RAF	17	28/5/9	FE
Laubman D C	RCAF	402	14+2sh/-/3	Eur
Mitchner J D	RCAF	416	10?/1+2sh/3	Eur
Moore L A	RCAF	402	3+3sh/1/1?	Eur
Morgan J M	RAF	208	7?/?/8	ME
Neil T F	RAF	41, 208	12+4sh/2/1	UK
Northcott G W	RCAF	126 Wg	8?/1/7?	Eur
Page A G	RAF	125 Wg	10+5sh/-/3	Eur
Pietrzak H	Pol	IFDF	7+2sh/1/1 & 4? V1	UK
Potoki W J	Pol	IFDF	4+2sh/-/1	UK
Russel B D	RCAF	126 Wg	2+5sh/2/4	Eur
Wilson C D M	RCAF	411	5/-/1	Eur
Winskill A L	RAF	17	4+2sh/1/1	Jap
Wojciechowski M I	Pol	2	4?/-/-	Eur

Notes

Those pilots with less than five victories or claims are marked thus * and are shown because of their inclusion in *Aces High* or *Those Other Eagles* where there may be doubt as to their actual scores

Theatre Abbreviations

UK - United Kingdom
Eur - Continental Europe
FE - Far East, India and Japan
ME - Mediterranean and Palestine

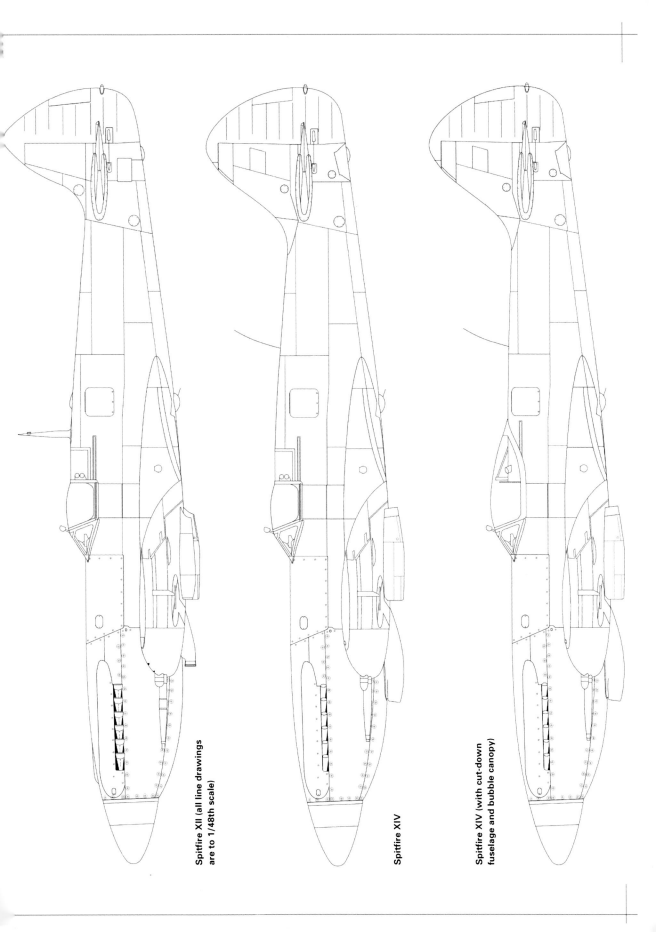

Spitfire XII (all line drawings are to 1/48th scale)

Spitfire XIV

Spitfire XIV (with cut-down fuselage and bubble canopy)

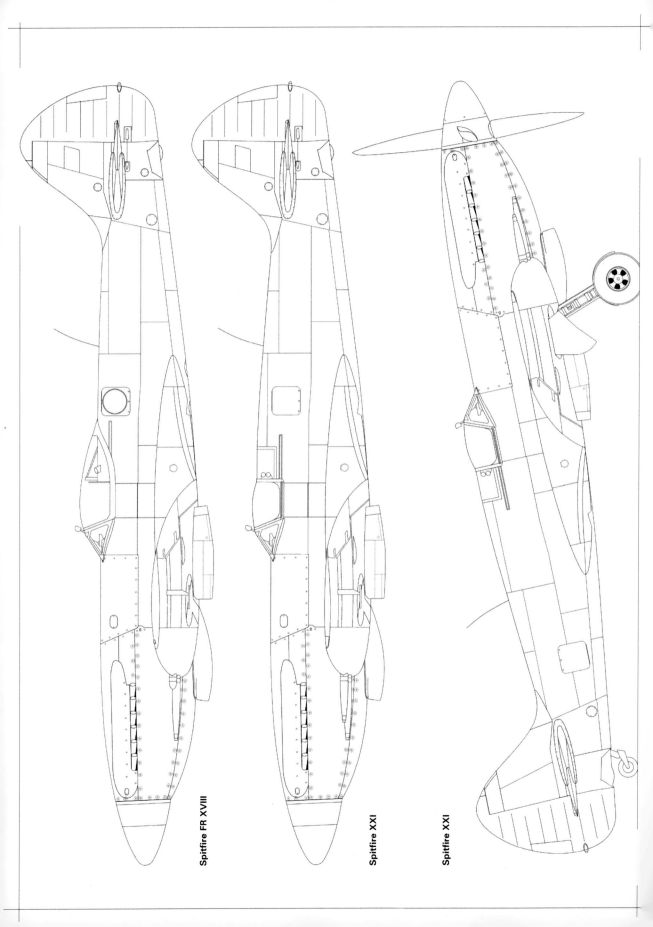

Spitfire FR XVIII

Spitfire XXI

Spitfire XXI

COLOUR PLATES

1

**Spitfire XII EN625/DL-K of Sqn Ldr R H Harries,
No 91 Sqn, Hawkinge, 25 May 1943**

By 25 May 1943, No 91 Sqn's CO, Sqn Ldr Ray Harries, had gained a total of seven victories, and was flying this aircraft during the Griffon-engined Spitfire's first big encounter with the Luftwaffe. As dusk fell, he was about to land at Hawkinge when a raid was reported heading towards Folkstone. Harries immediately led his patrol to engage the German aircraft, and in the subsequent fight over the Channel in rapidly failing light he was credited with two Fw 190s destroyed. He went on to claim a further nine victories with the Griffon Spitfire, thus becoming the most successful ace to fly this variant. EN625 was also used by Flg Off Ray Nash to destroy an Fw 190 and a Bf 109G later in the year. The fighter it was eventually written off in a forced landing on 11 December when the starboard wing was torn off.

2

**Spitfire XII EN620/DL-M of Flt Lt G Stenborg, No 91 Sqn,
Westhampnett, 23 September 1943**

EN620 had a successful career beginning on 24 August 1943 when its pilot on this occasion, Flg Off W G Mart, shared in the destruction of an enemy fighter with, amongst others, 11-victory Malta ace Flt Lt Gray Stenborg. A few days later Australian Flt Sgt 'Red' Blumer used it to claim the first of his 3.5 victories when he shot down an Fw 190 near Lille. Gray Stenborg was at the controls of EN620 on 23 September during a bomber escort mission when, to the northeast of Rouen, he shot down a Bf 109G. This was the young New Zealander's 15th, and final, victory, as he was shot down and killed during another escort sortie the following day. EN620, however, later transferred to No 41 Sqn, and survived the war only to be scrapped in 1946.

3

**Spitfire XII MB839/DL-V of Lt J Andrieux, No 91 Sqn,
Westhampnett and Tangmere, September-November 1943**

Twenty-six-year-old French pilot 'Jaco' Andrieux had escaped to Britain by boat in December 1940, and he later joined Spitfire-equipped No 130 Sqn, with whom he claimed his first victory. He transferred to No 91 Sqn in April 1943, and through the autumn regularly flew MB839 on operations over his native France. Indeed, he was in this aircraft when he downed a Bf 109G near Beaumont-le-Roger on 16 September. Three days later, Wg Cdr Ray Harries also used it to claim a victory. The Frenchman was again at its controls, when on 18 October, he brought down an Fw 190 near Amiens – he also claimed a probable in MB839 a month later. Andrieux became an ace during the summer of 1944 when serving with a Free French Spitfire squadron, but EN839 had by then been destroyed in a crash (on 24 April 1944).

4

**Spitfire XIV NH700/VL-P of Maj K C Kuhlmann,
No 322 (Dutch) Sqn, Acklington, March 1944**

Perhaps because of his Dutch ancestry, Maj Keith Kuhlmann of the SAAF was given command of the Dutch-manned No 322 Sqn in September 1943. He was still at the helm when, in March 1944, the unit began re-equipping with Spitfire XIVs. Kuhlmann (who had a total of eight claims, including four destroyed, from his service in Malta) was allocated NH700, which arrived on 14 March, as his personal mount. He flew it for the first time three days later, and it was adorned with his rank pennant and the Dutch inverted orange triangle marking. The aircraft did not survive for long, however, as on 11 April it crashed with the loss of Flg Off van Arkel. Kuhlmann led his unit with distinction in the battle against the V1s, personally destroying two of the missiles.

5

**Spitfire XII MB882/EB-B of Flt Lt D S Smith, No 41 Sqn,
Friston, April 1944**

MB882 was the last Spitfire XII built, and it joined No 41 Sqn in December 1943. On 26 March 1944 it had a narrow escape when Flg Off Peter Cowell, who subsequently gained four victories in Griffon Spitfires, bounced off the surface of the sea during a low level mission, damaging the fighter's propeller. MB882 was the mount of 'A' Flight commander, and Australian ace, Flt Lt Don Smith, at the time. With 4.5 kills to his name, Smith eventually left the squadron to command an Australian unit, whilst MB882 continued to fly with No 41 Sqn through the summer of 1944. Finally, on 3 September V1 ace Flt Lt Terry Spencer used it to shoot down an Fw 190 – the Spitfire XII's final (and his own sole) victory.

6

**Spitfire XIV NH654/DL-? of Flt Lt J-M Maridor, No 91 Sqn,
West Malling, 5 July 1944**

Having completed his training in England after the fall of France, 24-year-old Jean-Marie Maridor eventually joined No 91 Sqn, with whom he enjoyed a successful career, making nine claims that included at least 3.5 (and possibly more) destroyed. Of these, two destroyed and one damaged came in the Spitfire XII. Having converted with the squadron to the Mk XIV, Maridor was active during the campaign against the V1 flying bomb, shooting down his first on 18 June. He destroyed his fifth, to become a V1 ace, on 5 July, and later in the day was piloting this Spitfire when he shot down his sixth near Canterbury. Maridor did not encounter another until 3 August, when, seeing a flying bomb heading towards a large hospital, he closed up with the V1 prior to opening fire so as to ensure that he destroyed the weapon. Maridor's aircraft was literally blown to pieces too when the missile exploded killing the Frenchman. Unlike the unfortunate Maridor, NH654 survived the war and was transferred to the Belgian Air Force.

7

**Spitfire XIV RB188/DL-K of Flt Lt H D Johnson, No 91 Sqn,
West Malling, July 1944**

One of the most successful Spitfire pilots during the V1 campaign with 13.5 destroyed was Flt Lt 'Johnny' Johnson, who had been flying with No 91 Sqn since 1942. His first victory was in this aircraft on 23 June when he shared a V1 near Uckfield, and he brought down another near Hawkhurst the next day again in RB188. A little over a week later Johnson destroyed three more in this aircraft, which carried the stunning nose art of a naked red-head (named *BRUMHILDE*) riding a V1. RB188 was used to bring down three more 'buzz bombs', including the first success for future V1 ace Flg Off Ken Collier, as well as Jean Maridor's fourth kills. The aircraft later served on the Continent with Nos 130 and 350 Sqns, and was eventually transferred to Thailand post-war.

8

Spitfire XIV RM693/MN-S of Sqn Ldr M L D Donnet, No 350 (Belgian) Sqn, Hawkinge, August 1944

Having made a spectacular escape to England in 1941, pre-war Belgian pilot Mike Donnet soon joined an RAF Spitfire squadron and made nine claims during 1942-43, including three destroyed. In March 1944 he assumed command of No 350 Sqn, which was one of the RAF's two Belgian units, and he was at the helm when re-equipment with Spitfire XIVs began in August. Flown by Flg Off Hoenaert, RM693 participated in No 350 Sqn's first Mk XIV operation on 10 August. Several successful pilots, including Sgts Emile Pauwels and Andre Kicq, subsequently flew it in combat. Donnet logged his first mission in RM693 on the afternoon of 25 August when he escorted bombers to Beauvais, following this up with a 'Rhubarb' to the Gand and Courtrai areas and then another sortie in the evening. He then flew it constantly over the next few weeks. RM693 was later transferred to No 41 Sqn, where it was used by Flg Off Eric Gray to destroy a pair of Fw 190D-9s near Teschendorf on 20 April 1945.

9

Spitfire XIV RM683/AE-N of Sqn Ldr W G Dodd, No 402 Sqn RCAF, Hawkinge, 26 August 1944

Malta ace Sqn Ldr Wilbert Dodd assumed command of No 402 Sqn in July 1944, and RM683 flew its first operation with the unit the following month when Flt Lt de Niverville participated in an anti V1 patrol in the Ashford area on the 10th. Dodd flew it for the first time on 26 August when he led a sweep of the Compiegne area during the late morning, but he failed to encounter the enemy. Dodd left the squadron in October, but RM683 continued in use, being flown by Flg Off Sherk when he destroyed an Fw 190 near Aachen on Christmas Day. The aircraft was also the mount of yet another of No 402 Sqn's successful COs in the form of 16-victory ace Sqn Ldr Don Laubman on the evening of 8 April 1945 during an uneventful patrol – he was shot down and became a PoW just a few days later, however. RM683 also survived the war and was eventually transferred to the Belgian Air Force.

10

Spitfire XII MB862/EB-E of Flt Lt W N Stowe, No 41 Sqn, Lympne, September 1944

Delivered to No 41 Sqn in August 1943, MB862 saw extensive service with the unit and was damaged in combat several times. During the summer of 1944 it became the regular aircraft of future Griffon Spitfire ace Canadian Bill Stowe. He made his first claim in a Mk XII on 3 September, but a week later MB862 was damaged in a wheels-up landing whilst being flown by New Zealander Wt Off Brian Weeds. This was No 41 Sqn's final Mk XII 'prang' on operations.

However, the damage was not terminal, and MB862 was repaired and later used on second line tasks by No 595 Sqn, before being scrapped in 1946.

11

Spitfire XIV RB159/DW-D of Sqn Ldr R A Newbery, No 610 'County of Chester' Sqn, Lympne, September 1944

Richard Newbery, who had eight claims, including three (or four) destroyed, was in command of No 610 Sqn when it became the first unit to convert to the Spitfire XIV at the beginning of 1944. Newbery was allocated RB159 during the summer, and he flew it regularly throughout the anti-V1 campaign, during which he personally destroyed eight missiles and shared in the destruction of two others. He later led the unit to the Continent, before ending his lengthy tour. RB159 also had a long career, later serving with Nos 350, 41 and 416 Sqns, before being scrapped in 1949.

12

Spitfire XIV RM655/AP-S of Plt Off G Lord, No 130 Sqn, B82 Grave, Holland, October 1944

Having initially served with both Nos 322 and 350 Sqns, RM655 was eventually transferred to No 130 Sqn and flew with the unit after its move to the Continent in late September 1944. Among the squadron's pilots at this time was Flg Off Geoff Lord, who soon after D-Day had been shot down and escaped through enemy lines back to his unit. Lord, who in the spring of 1945 became an ace flying the Spitfire XIV, first flew RM655 on 6 October when, during an armed reconnaissance to the Wesel area, he destroyed an enemy truck. He again flew this aircraft the next day on an uneventful high level patrol of Nijmegen. After lengthy operational use, RM655 was struck off charge just before the end of the war.

13

Spitfire XIV RM787/CG of Wg Cdr C Gray, Lympne Wing, Lympne, October 1944

With 27 and two shared victories to his name, Wg Cdr Colin Gray was the most successful New Zealand fighter pilot of World War 2. On 11 August 1944 he arrived to command the Spitfire XIV-equipped Lympne Wing, and was allocated RM787 as his personal mount. In keeping with the privilege of his position, the fighter was quickly adorned with his initials. After participating in the latter stages of the V1 campaign, during which, to his frustration, he was unable to engage any flying bombs, in the autumn Gray's wing began long-range bomber escorts to German targets. With little sign of the Luftwaffe, however, he was unable to increase his total. RM787 was later transferred to No 130 Sqn, and after the war, like many other Mk XIVs, it was acquired by the Belgian Air Force and given the serial SG28.

14

Spitfire XIV RM675 of Wt Off F E F Edwards, No 130 Sqn, B82 Grave, Holland, 3 October 1944

Australian Freddie Edwards joined No 130 Sqn shortly after D-Day and first saw action in the Spitfire XIV during the V1 campaign, when he shared in the destruction of a flying bomb. He moved with No 130 Sqn to the Continent in late

September and flew RM675, which although still carrying AEAF identity stripes was devoid of unit code letters, on a high level patrol over the Arnhem area on 3 October. Edwards remained with No 130 Sqn until the end of the war, finding no success until the final two weeks of the conflict when, in an eight-day period, he claimed six victories. RM675 was not so lucky, however, as on 25 April 1945 it caught fire while taking off from Celle and was destroyed..

15

Spitfire XIV RM862/AE-K of Sqn Ldr L A Moore, No 402 Sqn RCAF, B88 Heesch, Holland, 28 February 1945

Leslie Moore, who was an American citizen serving in the RCAF, achieved acedom in the weeks after D-Day, and in February 1945 he returned to No 402 Sqn as CO. Engaged on armed reconnaissance missions over enemy territory, he first flew RM862, which was the regular aircraft of Flt Lt Ken Sleep, during the morning of 28 February on a sweep to the Munster area. Moore used it again on 3 March on a mission towards Emmerich. Sadly, he was killed when attacking a train on 25 March. RM862 was also flown by another of No 402 Sqn's COs, 11-victory ace Sqn Ldr Don Gordon, who flew two sweeps in it on 19 April. The aircraft survived the war, and like many of its contemporaries, later served in the reconstituted Belgian Air Force.

16

Spitfire XIV NH745/EB-V of Sqn Ldr D I Benham, No 41 Sqn, B78 Eindhoven, Holland, March-April 1945

One of the first Spitfire XIVs to be fitted with the 'bubble' canopy, NH745 was issued to No 41 Sqn in late March 1945. For a short time it was the personal mount of the unit's CO, Sqn Ldr Douglas Benham, who had achieved ace status in North Africa and claimed his final two victories flying the Spitfire XIV in January 1945. In addition to his rank pennant, Benham's aircraft also carried a small squadron badge on the nose – an unusual addition for the period. Benham's tour ended in early April, but NH745 did not survive long after this as it was badly damaged when it hit an object while taking off from Rheine on the 16th and it was not repaired.

17

Spitfire XIV SM826/EB-B of Sqn Ldr J B Shepherd, No 41 Sqn, B106 Twente, Holland, 14 April 1945

John Shepherd was flying this aircraft on a sweep north of Bremen on 14 April when, near the airfield of Nordholz, he shot down a Bf 110 that was towing an Me 163 rocket fighter. Credited with both destroyed, these were the first of his eight victories scored on Griffon Spitfires. SM826 was itself an ace aircraft, as in addition to Shepherd's two victories, it was flown in several other successful actions. On 17 April Flg Off Hegarty had destroyed a Ju 88 over Lubeck with it, and on 25 April Flg Off Pat Coleman, who also became an ace, shared in the destruction of another Ju 88 whilst flying SM826. Three days later he also shared an He 111 kill during a mission in this aircraft, and during another sortie that same day, Australian ace Flt Lt Tony Gaze used SM826 to help bring down an Fw 190D-9 over Lake Schwerin airfield. SM826 also took part in No 41 Sqn's final war patrol when flown by Flg Off Farfan on 5 May. Following post-war service, it became an instructional airframe in December 1948.

18

Spitfire XIV MV260/EB-P of Flt Lt P Cowell, No 41 Sqn, B118 Celle, Germany, April 1945

MV260 was another 'bubble-hooded' Spitfire XIV that was flown in the closing weeks of the war by a number of No 41 Sqn's successful pilots. It also took part in several successful combats, with Flt Lt R R Fisher using it to destroy an Fw 190. For much of April MV260 was the regular mount of Flt Lt Peter Cowell, who was to end the war with four victories to his name. Other successful pilots who flew it were Flg Off Eric Gray, who also had four victories, and Flt Lt Derek Rake, while the CO, John Shepherd and fellow aces Flt Lts Bill Stowe and John Wilkinson also flew MV260 during April. Post-war, during the May-June period, and before its transfer to No 416 Sqn, it was also regularly flown by Flt Lt Tony Gaze.

19

Spitfire XIV MV263/GCK of Wg Cdr G C Keefer, No 125 Wing, B106 Twente, Holland, and B118 Celle, Germany, April 1945

One of the most distinguished Canadian pilots of World War 2 was the No 125 Wing leader, George Keefer, who, during the final weeks of the war, usually led his wing in this aircraft, which as was usual at the time carried his initials and rank pennant. His first claim in the 'bubble-hooded' MV263 was on 16 April when, in a combat over Hagenow airfield, he damaged an Fw 190. Two days later, in an armed reconnaissance, Keefer destroyed five Bf 109s on the ground at Parchim. On 20 April he shot down a Bf 109, and on the 25th he downed an Fw 190 near Pritzwalk as his 12th, and last, victim – it was also his fourth with the Mk XIV. Like its pilot, MV263 survived the war and later served in Belgium as SG77.

20

Spitfire XIV RB155/MN-C of Plt Off D J Watkins, No 350 (Belgian) Sqn, B118 Celle, Germany, 20 April 1945

Des Watkins was one of a number of pilots who became an ace flying Spitfire XIVs during the final weeks of the war. A Briton serving with a Belgian squadron, he achieved his first victory at the controls of this aircraft when, during a sweep over Berlin on 20 April, he shot down an Fw 190. RB155 had, however, already seen a successful combat, as over Hamburg three days earlier, Flt Sgt Andre Kicq claimed the first of his three victories when he shot down a Bf 109. He was also flying it when he shared in the destruction of an Ar 234 jet on 2 May – the same shared victory that took Des Watkins to acedom. RB155 also saw post-war service as an instructional airframe with the Royal Netherlands Air Force.

21

Spitfire XIV RM931/EB-U of Flt Lt J F Wilkinson, No 41 Sqn, B18 Celle, Germany, 20 April 1945

RM931 had originally served with No 610 Sqn, and after the unit's disbandment it was transferred to No 41 Sqn, which was engaged in offensive sweeps over the remaining enemy territory. It was flown by Flt Lt John Wilkinson, who had achieved his first victory a few days earlier, during one such mission over the Oranienburg area on 20 April. At around 0730 hrs during the course of this operation, the No 41 Sqn formation attacked a number of Fw 190s. In one engagement

APPENDICES

93

Wilkinson shared the destruction of a Focke-Wulf fighter with his CO, Sqn Ldr John Shepherd. Almost immediately, he then attacked another, and was credited with sharing its demise with Flt Sgt P F Scott. A week later Wilkinson was elevated to ace status. RM931 did not long survive the war, as it suffered an engine failure when taking off from Vaerlose on 1 July and was wrecked in the subsequent crash.

22

Spitfire XXI LA223/DL-Y of Flt Lt J W P Draper, No 91 Sqn, Ludham, April 1945

One of the more unusual combat claims made by a Griffon Spitfire was that submitted by Canadian ace (and Griffon Spitfire V1 ace) Flt Lt John Draper. A long serving member of No 91 Sqn, he was still with the unit when, in April 1945, it was re-equipped with Spitfire XXIs and began patrolling the Dutch coast from its Norfolk base in search of enemy midget submarines. Early on the 26th, flying LA223 (his usual mount), Draper set out with another aircraft for the Dutch coast on an anti-submarine operation. Shortly after midday, the pair spotted a midget submarine (probably a *Biber*) off the Hook of Holland. They immediately attacked, obtaining strikes around the conning tower, and after a second strafe it was seen to sink, giving Draper a most unusual final combat claim!

23

Spitfire XIV NH689/MN-B of Flt Sgt G F Gigot, No 350 (Belgian) Sqn, B118 Celle, Germany, 30 April 1945

This was the usual mount of No 350 Sqn's CO and V1 ace Sqn Ldr Terry Spencer, but it was also flown by a number of other successful pilots, including ace Plt Off Des Watkins and Flt Lt Pat Bangerter, who ended with four victories and five V1s. It was in the hands of Flt Sgt Guy Gigot when, on 30 April, the aircraft encountered a group of Fw 190s in the Lake Schwerin area. In the subsequent combat, the 23-year-old Belgian shot down one German fighter and shared in the destruction of another to take his total to four. After the war NH689 was transferred to No 443 Sqn, and it later became an instructional airframe.

24

Spitfire XIV MV264/EB-Q of Flg Off E Gray, No 41 Sqn, B118 Celle, Germany, 1 May 1945

Another of No 41 Sqn's 'bubble hood' Spitfire XIVs, MV264 was also flown by several successful pilots. Amongst them was Flg Off Eric Gray, who, during a sweep to the Lake Schwerin area on 1 May, shared in the destruction of a long-nosed Fw 190D-9 with his CO, John Shepherd, thus taking his tally to four destroyed. Two days earlier it had been flown in another successful action by Flg Off Pat Coleman, who shared in the destruction of an He 111, and later that same day ace Flt Lt John Wilkinson had also sortied in it. MV264 moved with the unit to Kastrup in the re-occupation of Denmark but it was subsequently written off in an accident that summer.

25

Spitfire FR XIV NH915/EB-H of Flt Lt D S V Rake, No 41 Sqn, B118 Celle, Germany, 3 May 1945

NH915 was the usual aircraft of Flt Lt Derek Rake, who was leading a patrol in it on 3 May when he caught a Ju 188 at very low level near Lubeck and shot it down. This was No 41 Sqn's 200th, and final, victory of the war. Two days later Rake, who had shared in the destruction of an Ar 234 some weeks before, was flying NH915 when he led the squadron's final patrol of the war, departing Celle at 0620 hrs. During early May, NH915 had also been flown by several of the squadron's notable pilots, including Sqn Ldr John Shepherd, Flt Lt Peter Cowell and Flg Off Eric Gray. After the war NH915 served with No 416 Sqn, before being struck off charge in 1946. Rake remained in the RAF, enjoying a distinguished post-war career.

26

Spitfire FR XIV NH903/VC-P of Sqn Ldr J B Prendergast, No 414 Sqn RCAF, B156 Luneburg, Germany, May 1945

In early 1945 the Spitfire XIV began being used by some 2nd TAF fighter reconnaissance units, including No 414 Sqn, one of whose pilots achieved acedom whilst flying the type on 2 May. Another of the unit's pilots to enjoy air combat success that day was unit CO Sqn Ldr Jim Prendergast, who, over Weismar harbour during an armed reconnaissance, shot down two Fw 190s to claim his only victories. After the end of the war some of the squadron's aircraft, including this one, adopted unit code letters, and Prendergast's personal mount also acquired this attractive nose art. NH903 remained with the RAF as part of the occupation forces until 1950.

27

Spitfire XIV MV257/JEJ of Gp Capt J E Johnson, No 125 Wing, Kastrup, Denmark, June 1945

With 34 and 7 shared victories, 'Johnnie' Johnson was the most successful RAF pilot in northwest Europe. He ended the war commanding No 125 Wing, which had moved to Denmark to reoccupy the country. He had long flown Spitfires with his initials, and with No 125 Wing, his post-war mount (MV257) discretely carried his JEJ monicker – it was the last Spitfire to be so marked. The aircraft had previously been used by George Keefer, and was flown by Johnson when he led a celebratory flypast over Copenhagen. Deemed to be battle-weary, MV257 was duly struck off charge at the end of June.

28

Spitfire XIV RN135/YB-A of Sqn Ldr J H Lacey, No 17 Sqn, Seletar, Singapore, September-December 1945

'Ginger' Lacey was one of the most famous RAF fighter pilots of World War 2, and he was also one of the leading aces of the Battle of Britain. Later posted to India for training duties, he eventually returned to operations flying Spitfires over Burma, and in November 1944 assumed command of No 17 Sqn, which he led with distinction. In June 1945 the squadron was re-equipped with Spitfire XIVEs in preparation for the assault on Malaya. After the Japanese surrender, No 17 Sqn was ferried by aircraft carrier to Singapore, where Lacey flew this aircraft. It was marked up with the squadron's mailed fist badge on the nose and Lacey's impressive scoreboard, showing victories over 27 German and one Japanese aircraft. When the squadron moved to Japan as part of the occupation force, it remained Lacey's mount, although the markings were changed somewhat. RN135 was scrapped in Japan after the RAF's withdrawal in 1948.

29

**Spitfire XIV MV263/JEFF of Wg Cdr G W Northcott,
No 126 Wing, B174 Utersen, Germany, September
1945-March 1946**

Having previously commanded No 402 Sqn, 8.5 victory ace
Wg Cdr Geoff Northcott later led the Spitfire-equipped No 126
Wing during the final months of World War 2, flying his
personally marked aircraft 'JEFF'. Northcott returned to
Canada during the summer of 1945, but in September he
returned to Germany, where he assumed leadership of the
wing once more. By this stage its Spitfire IX squadrons had
largely re-equipped with Spitfire XIVs, and MV263 became
his personal mount. The fighter carried his initials to identify
its assignment to the wing leader. Northcott remained in
command until the Wing disbanded in March 1946. MV263
was later transferred to the Belgian Air Force, serving with
the *Ecole de Chasse* until crashing in 1950.

30

**Spitfire XIV RN133/FF-B of Sqn Ldr K L Charney,
No 132 Sqn, Kai Tak, Hong Kong, February 1946**

Ken Charney assumed command of No 132 Sqn in the
summer of 1944, and led his squadron through the campaign
in Normandy, taking his final score to six destroyed, all on
Spitfires. During the autumn No 132 was ordered to the
Far East, eventually arriving in India in early 1945, where it
received Spitfires once more. In May the unit re-equipped
with Spitfire XIVs in preparation for the invasion of Malaya.
However, the abrupt ending of the war with Japan made this
unnecessary. Thus, in September, No 132 Sqn was
ferried by aircraft carrier to re-occupy Hong Kong. This aircraft
was allocated to Sqn Ldr Charney, who flew it on local
defence and anti-piracy patrols until his squadron disbanded in
April 1946. RN133 later served in Japan with the Occupation
Force.

31

**Spitfire FR 18 TZ203/RG-J of Sqn Ldr C F Ambrose,
No 208 Sqn, Ein Shemer, Palestine, September 1947**

Charles Ambrose amassed eight claims during World War 2,
including 2.5 destroyed during his service in the Battle of
Britain and over the desert. In May 1947 he was given
command of No 208 Sqn, which was based in Palestine and
engaged in policing duties in attempts to suppress militant
Jewish organisations. Ambrose flew this aircraft, which was
adorned with a large squadron badge, during the later part of
1947. The following year several of No 208 Sqn's Spitfire
FR 18s were shot down by Israeli fighters.

32

**Spitfire FR 18 NH850/Z of Sqn Ldr W G G Duncan-Smith,
No 60 Sqn, Kuala Lumpur, Malaya, 31 December 1950**

In July 1949, one of the RAF's most successful Spitfire pilots,
19-victory ace Sqn Ldr Wilf Duncan-Smith, was made CO of
Singapore-based No 60 Sqn. His unit was heavily engaged in
strike operations in support of the campaign against
Communist terrorists in Malaya. On 31 December 1950, flying
this machine as section leader for three other fighters on the
last occasion when an RAF Spitfire fired its guns in anger,
they attacked a terrorist hideout near Kota Tinggi with rocket
projectiles. This was the last of 1800 Spitfire attack sorties

flown during Operation *Firedog*. Duncan-Smith also led the
RAF's first jet strike soon afterwards too. His Spitfire is
adorned with yellow and black nose stripes, a blue/red
spinner – unique to the CO's aircraft – and his rank pennant,
as well as No 60 Sqn's markhor's head badge on its fin.

BIBLIOGRAPHY

Bowyer, Michael, *Fighting Colours.* PSL, 1969 and 1975

Cull, Brian & Aloni, Shlomo with Nicolle, David, *Spitfires
over Israel.* Grub St, 1997

Donnet, Baron Michael, *Flight to Freedom.* Wingham Press,
1991

Flintham, Vic & Thomas, Andrew, *Combat Codes.* Airlife,
2003

Griffin, John & Kostenuk, Samuel, *RCAF Squadron
Histories & Aircraft.* Samuel Stevens, 1977

Halley, James, *Squadrons of the RAF & Commonwealth.* Air
Britain, 1988

Herrington, John, *Australian in the War 1939-45, Series 3
Volume 3.* Halstead Press, 1962

Hunt, Leslie, *Twenty One Squadrons.* Garnstone Press, 1972

Jefford, Wg Cdr C G, *RAF Squadrons.* Airlife 1988 and 2001

Lee, Sir David, *Eastward.* HMSO, 1984

Lee, Sir David, *Wings in the Sun.* HMSO, 1989

Listemann, Philippe, Tilley P-A & Eherengardt, C-J, *Les
Pilotes de chasse Francaise.* Aero Editions, 1999

Milberry, Larry & Halliday, Hugh, *The Royal Canadian Air
Force at War 1939-1945.* CANAV Books, 1990

Rawlings, John D R, *Fighter Squadrons of the RAF.*
Macdonald, 1969

Richards, Denis, *RAF Official History 1939-45, Parts 2 & 3.*
HMSO, 1954

Robertson, Bruce, *Spitfire, The story of a Famous Fighter.*
Harleyford, 1960

Shores, Christopher, *Aces High Vol 2.* Grub St, 1999

Shores, Christopher, *Those Other Eagles.* Grub St, 2004

Shores, Christopher & Thomas, Chris, *2nd Tactical Air
Force Vols 2 & 3.* Classic, 2005 & 2006

Shores, Christopher & Williams, Clive, *Aces High Vol 1.*
Grub St, 1994

ACKNOWLEDGEMENTS

The author wishes to record his gratitude to the following
former Spitfire pilots and relatives who have given of their
time in answering queries and presenting accounts for
inclusion within this volume – the late Sqn Ldr J M V
Carpenter DFC & bar, Gp Capt D S V Rake OBE AFC,
Wg Cdr A G Todd DFC and G L Watkins Esq (son of the
late D J Watkins DFC).

INDEX

References to illustrations are shown in **bold**. Plates are shown with page and caption locators in brackets.